Going Back In Time

Daily Life

Day 1

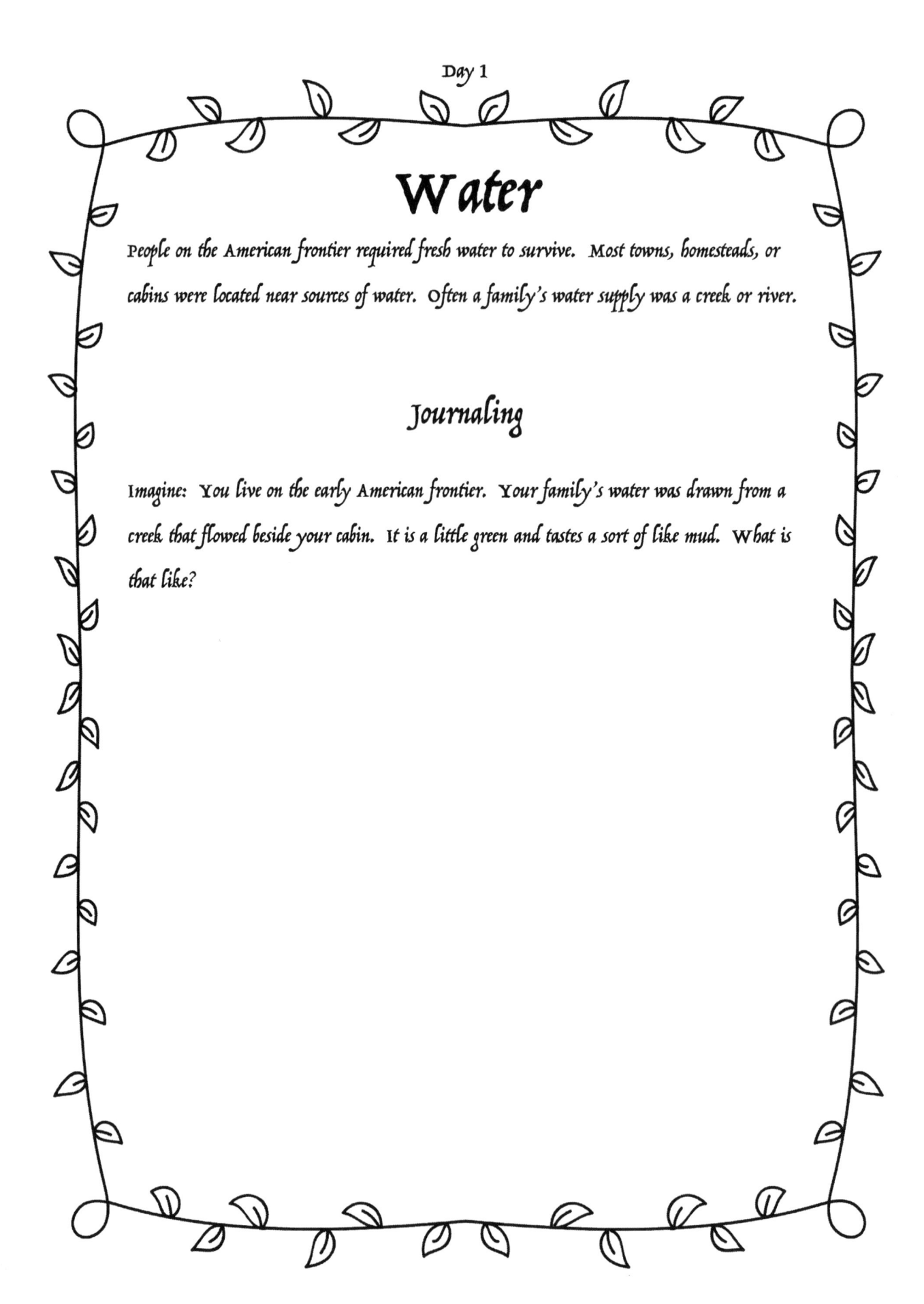

Water

People on the American frontier required fresh water to survive. Most towns, homesteads, or cabins were located near sources of water. Often a family's water supply was a creek or river.

Journaling

Imagine: You live on the early American frontier. Your family's water was drawn from a creek that flowed beside your cabin. It is a little green and tastes a sort of like mud. What is that like?

My Colonial Journal For Girls

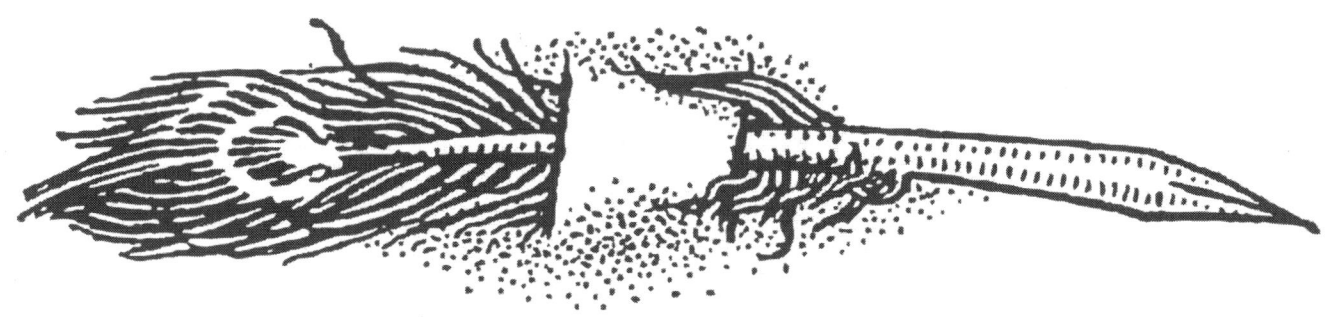

by

Geoff Baggett

Copyright © 2017 Geoff Baggett

All rights reserved.

ISBN: 0-9973833-7-2
ISBN-13: 978-0-9973833-7-9

Combining Journaling and History

Journaling is fun! It is a great way to record your thoughts, ideas, and feelings. It provides an opportunity for you to tell your personal story. It unleashes your unique creativity. It can also help you discover a love for writing. Many students today are familiar with journaling. They have experienced journaling exercises in the classroom, often times at the beginning of the school day. It helps get your thinking and "creative juices" going.

Unfortunately, many young people today know very little about our nation's history, especially the Colonial and Revolutionary War periods. I want to help change that! I want to help you discover more about the Colonial Period in our American History (before 1776) and the time of the American Revolutionary War (1776-1783). MY COLONIAL JOURNAL is a unique and fun educational tool that combines writing with history and learning. It is a 50-day journey through time that helps you connect personally with the very difficult and challenging experience of life in early America.

As you progress through your copy of MY COLONIAL JOURNAL, you will likely encounter topics and themes that seem to be difficult and grim. I want you to understand that it was an extremely troubling time in our American history. Everyone, including children, suffered tremendously during the time period. You may also encounter a few words or other concepts that seem unfamiliar. In a few cases, you may even have to ask an adult about something or search online for information. That is okay. Do not get frustrated. You actually need to develop skills in research and finding answers to your questions. Plus, when you "dig deeper," you will also learn more about your American history!

So ... get ready to experience a very historical Colonial and Revolutionary adventure as you explore your own thoughts and feelings. Enjoy yourself. Be creative. And most of all, have fun!

Geoff Baggett

Day 1

Water

Day 2

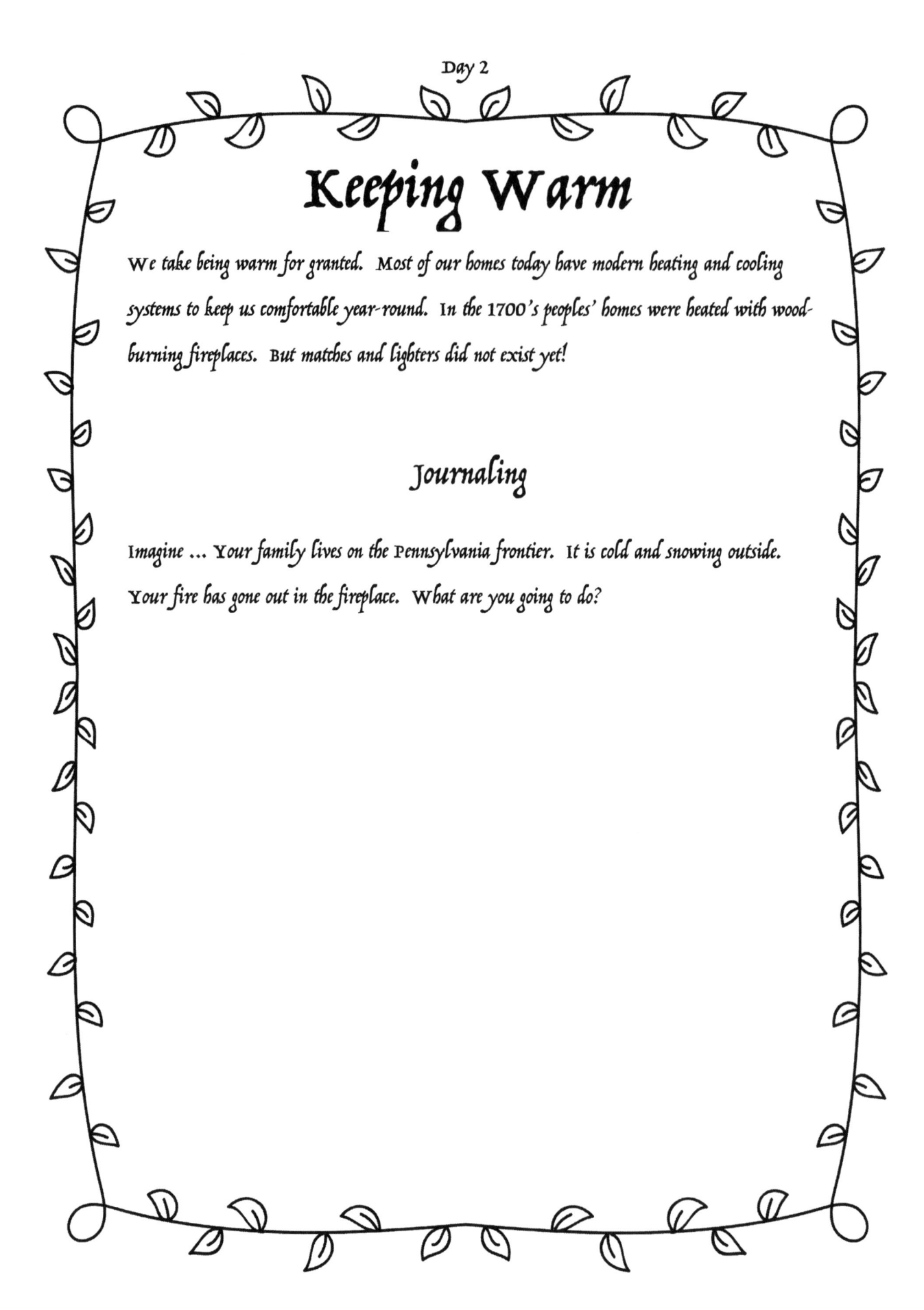

Keeping Warm

We take being warm for granted. Most of our homes today have modern heating and cooling systems to keep us comfortable year-round. In the 1700's peoples' homes were heated with wood-burning fireplaces. But matches and lighters did not exist yet!

Journaling

Imagine ... Your family lives on the Pennsylvania frontier. It is cold and snowing outside. Your fire has gone out in the fireplace. What are you going to do?

Day 2

Keeping Warm

Draw a picture of a big colonial fireplace with a toasty fire.

Day 3

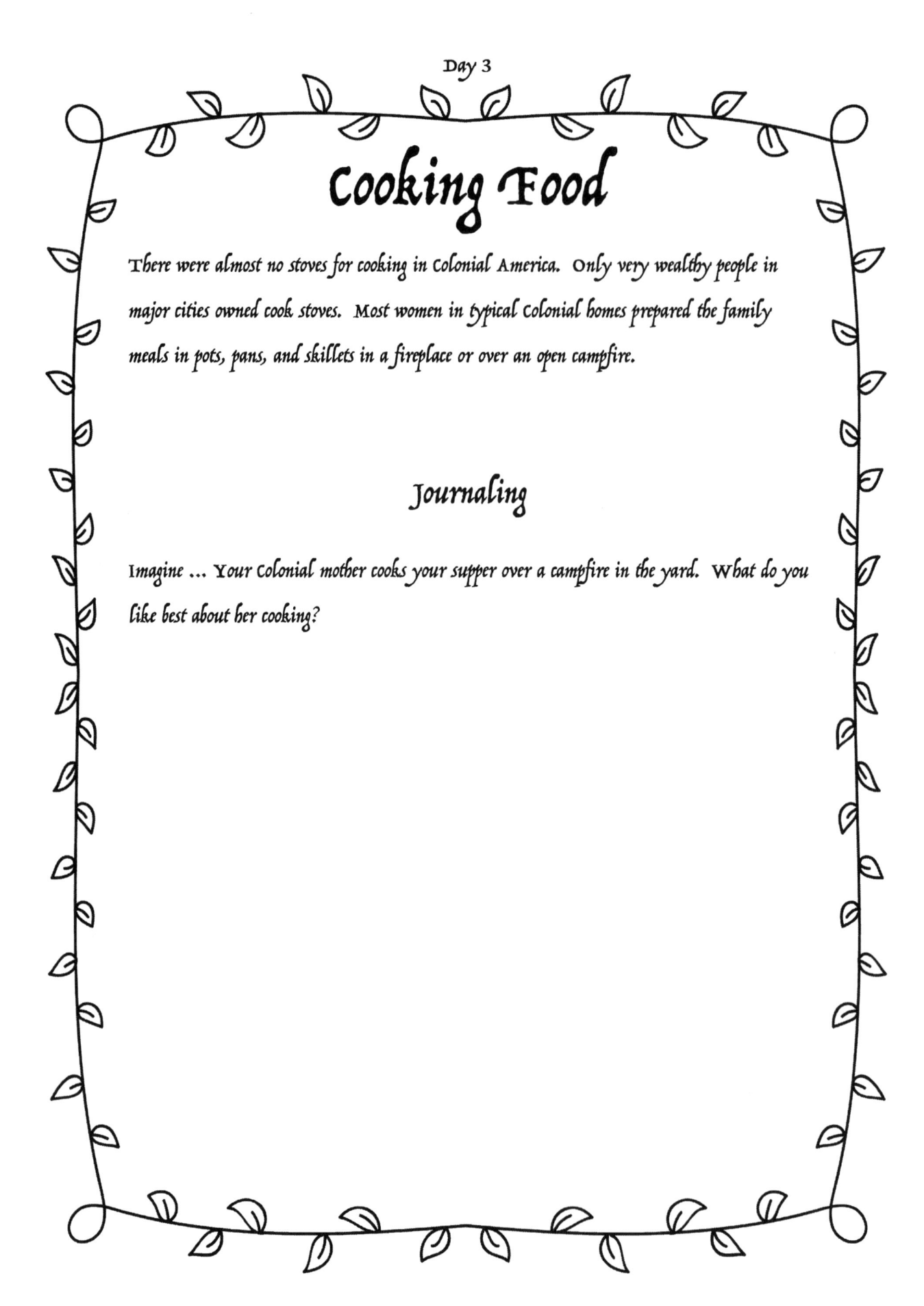

Cooking Food

There were almost no stoves for cooking in Colonial America. Only very wealthy people in major cities owned cook stoves. Most women in typical colonial homes prepared the family meals in pots, pans, and skillets in a fireplace or over an open campfire.

Journaling

Imagine ... Your Colonial mother cooks your supper over a campfire in the yard. What do you like best about her cooking?

Day 3

Do a little research online about things that people ate during colonial times. Make a list of common foods that people ate.

Day 4

Diary Day

Pretend that you are living in Colonial America. Try to imagine yourself living during that time. Now ... write two diary pages as a colonial girl. Reflect on the things you have already learned about the everyday life of a colonial girl.

Day 4

Diary Day

Day 5

Choose an Outfit!

Clothing was very expensive in the 1700's. Cloth had to be made by hand on a loom or imported from Europe. Even buttons were very expensive and difficult to purchase. Most people in Colonial America only owned one or two outfits to wear! That is all! One or two outfits!

Journaling

Think about all of the items of clothing that you own. Your closet and drawers are probably full of garments. Now ... imagine that they are all gone, and you could only have one outfit. That's it! No more! You own no other items of clothing. You must wear this outfit every single day. Which outfit would you choose and why? Describe it in every detail.

Day 5

Choose an Outfit!

Day 6

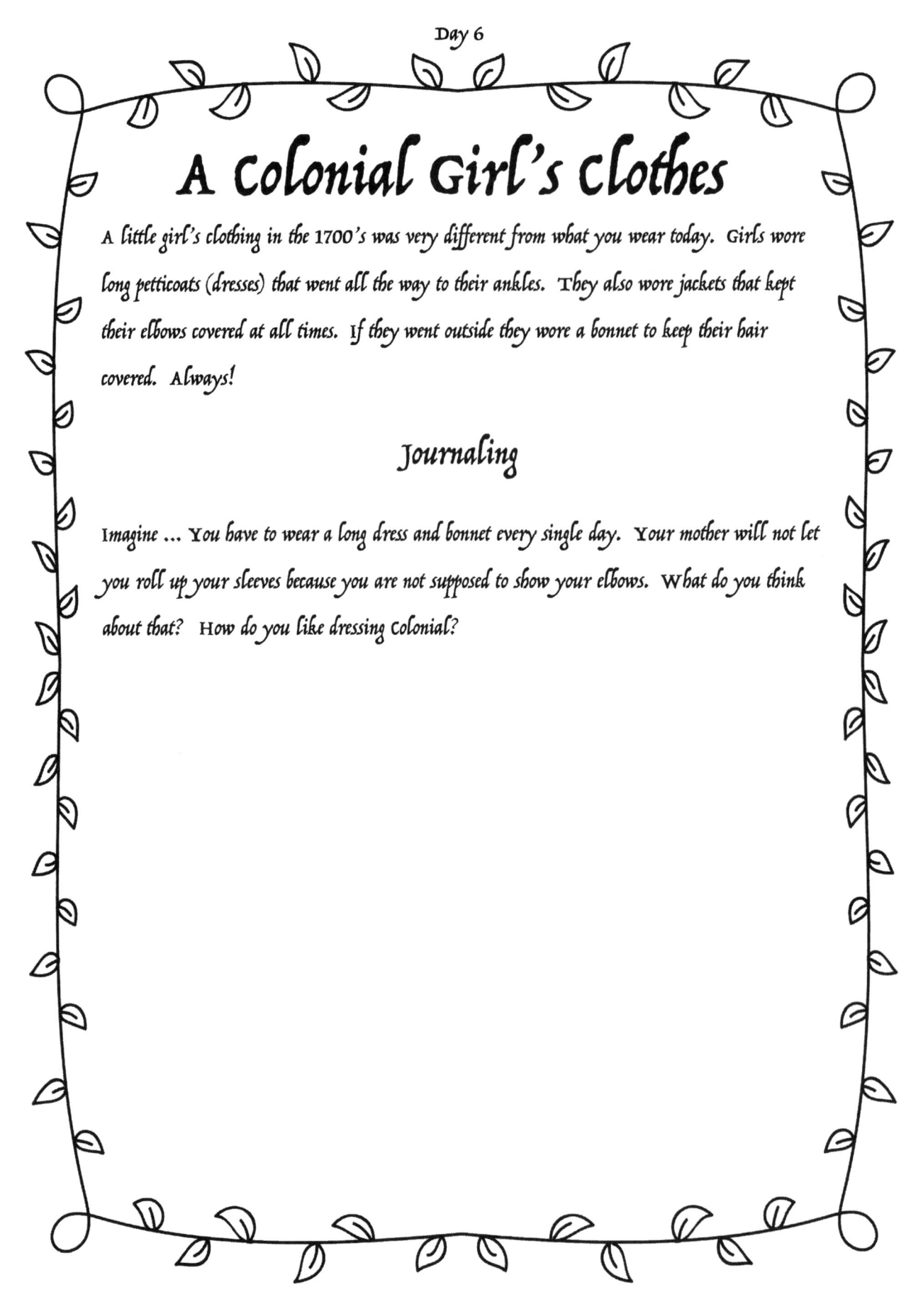

A Colonial Girl's Clothes

A little girl's clothing in the 1700's was very different from what you wear today. Girls wore long petticoats (dresses) that went all the way to their ankles. They also wore jackets that kept their elbows covered at all times. If they went outside they wore a bonnet to keep their hair covered. Always!

Journaling

Imagine ... You have to wear a long dress and bonnet every single day. Your mother will not let you roll up your sleeves because you are not supposed to show your elbows. What do you think about that? How do you like dressing Colonial?

Day 6

A Colonial Girl's Clothes

Draw a picture of a girl in Colonial clothing. When you're finished, cut out a picture of your face and paste it on the Colonial Girl.

Hint ~ You can find lots of images online. Ask an adult in your life to help you search on Google or Yahoo.

Day 7

Colonial Money

Ordinary families in Colonial America had very little money. Most communities operated on a barter system. People traded goods and services for things of equal value. Occasionally some of the colonies issued paper money and coins. But mostly the coins that were used in America came from other coins. There were British pennies and half-pennies, Spanish silver dollars, and French silver coins. Sometimes, to make change with silver dollars, people cut them into little pie-shaped pieces!

Journaling

Imagine that there was no money used in America today. People simply trade things or do jobs to earn necessities and supplies. What skills or jobs could you offer that could earn things for your family?

Day 7

Colonial Money

Draw a picture of a Spanish 8-Reale Coin (Spanish Silver Dollar).

Draw the various sized pieces that people might cut from them.

Hint ~ You can find excellent information by searching on Google for "Cutting a Spanish Silver Dollar."

Day 8

Strange Shoes and No Shoes

When you were little, did you ever put your shoes on backwards? You know ... on the wrong feet? Of course, now you know which shoe goes on your left foot and which one goes on your right foot by the shape of each shoe. Our shoes always curve toward the inside ... toward the middle.

In the 1700's there was no such thing as a right shoe or left shoe! Every shoe was shaped exactly the same! They were called "straight-lasted." Most were made of black leather and held in place on the foot by a large brass buckle. Little girls and boys would often have to make a mark on the inside of their shoes to know which foot to wear them on. Sadly, many boys and girls had no shoes. Poor people often went bare-footed, even in the winter!

Journaling

Imagine ... You live on the Virginia frontier. The year is 1772. A storm destroyed your family's tobacco crop. Your Papa has no more money and cannot afford to buy you any shoes for the winter. What will you do? What can you use for shoes?

Day 8

Strange Shoes and No Shoes

Day 9

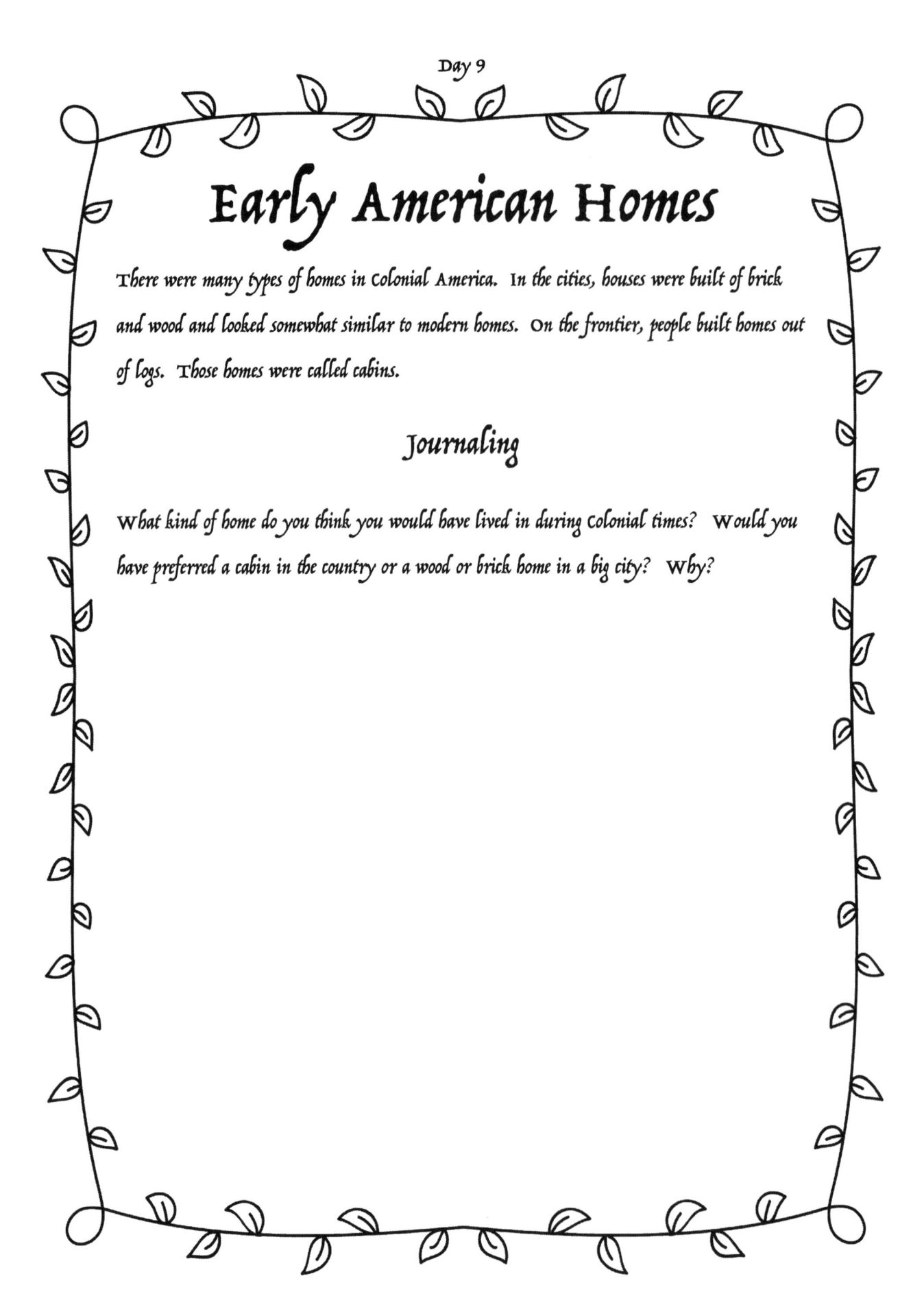

Early American Homes

There were many types of homes in Colonial America. In the cities, houses were built of brick and wood and looked somewhat similar to modern homes. On the frontier, people built homes out of logs. Those homes were called cabins.

Journaling

What kind of home do you think you would have lived in during Colonial times? Would you have preferred a cabin in the country or a wood or brick home in a big city? Why?

Day 9

Early American Homes

Draw a picture of your imaginary Colonial home.

Day 10

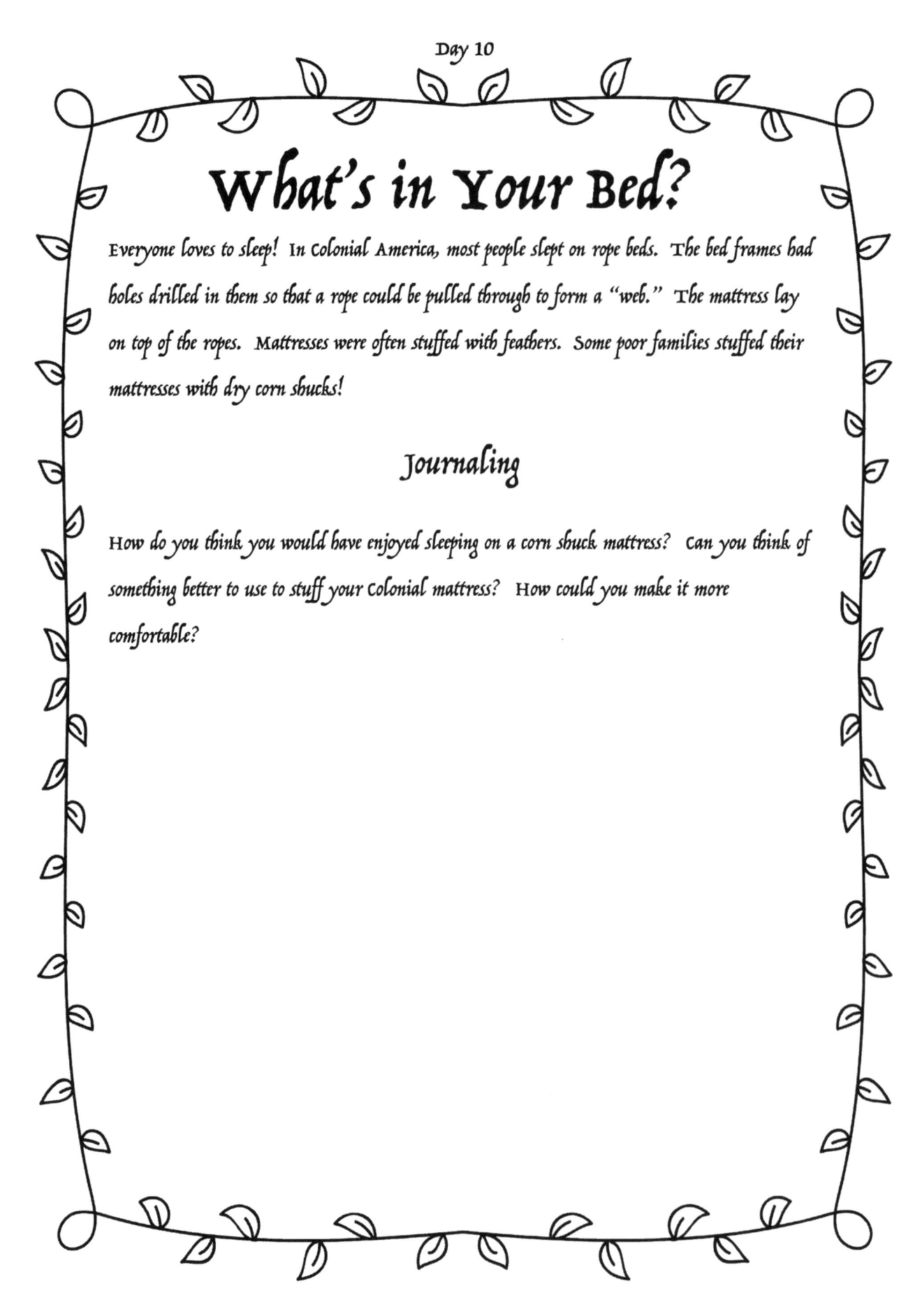

What's in Your Bed?

Everyone loves to sleep! In Colonial America, most people slept on rope beds. The bed frames had holes drilled in them so that a rope could be pulled through to form a "web." The mattress lay on top of the ropes. Mattresses were often stuffed with feathers. Some poor families stuffed their mattresses with dry corn shucks!

Journaling

How do you think you would have enjoyed sleeping on a corn shuck mattress? Can you think of something better to use to stuff your Colonial mattress? How could you make it more comfortable?

Day 10

What's in Your Bed?

Day 11

Light for Nighttime

After the sun goes down each evening, we light up our homes by flipping the light switch. Light bulbs brighten our nighttime world with a light almost as bright as the daylight. In the 1700's people usually went to bed shortly after sundown. They slept when it was dark and stayed awake when it was light.

Journaling

Imagine: Your Mama and Papa make you go to sleep as soon as the sun goes down each day. Every day you wake up when the rooster crows in the morning. What will you do before sunset on this Colonial day?

Day 11

Light for Nighttime

Draw something that would have been used to light up a house in Colonial America.

Day 12

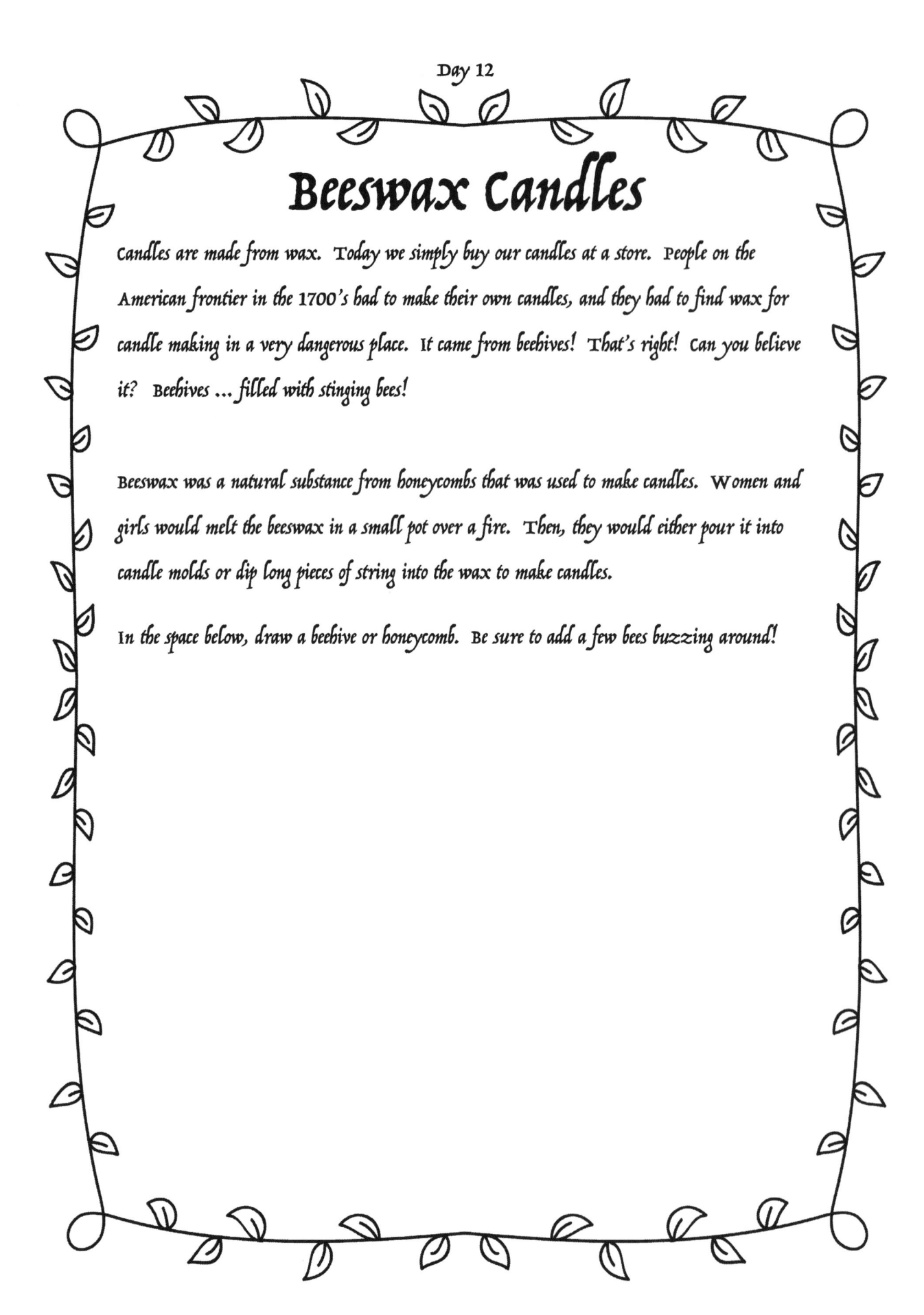

Beeswax Candles

Candles are made from wax. Today we simply buy our candles at a store. People on the American frontier in the 1700's had to make their own candles, and they had to find wax for candle making in a very dangerous place. It came from beehives! That's right! Can you believe it? Beehives ... filled with stinging bees!

Beeswax was a natural substance from honeycombs that was used to make candles. Women and girls would melt the beeswax in a small pot over a fire. Then, they would either pour it into candle molds or dip long pieces of string into the wax to make candles.

In the space below, draw a beehive or honeycomb. Be sure to add a few bees buzzing around!

Day 12

Beeswax Candles

Journaling

You have to collect honey and beeswax from a beehive on your family farm. How can you do that without getting stung?

Day 13

Diary Day

It's our weekly diary day! Pretend that you are living in Colonial America. Try to imagine yourself living during that time. Now ... write two diary pages as a Colonial girl. Reflect on the things you have learned over the past week about the colonial life of a young girl.

Day 13

Diary Day

Day 14

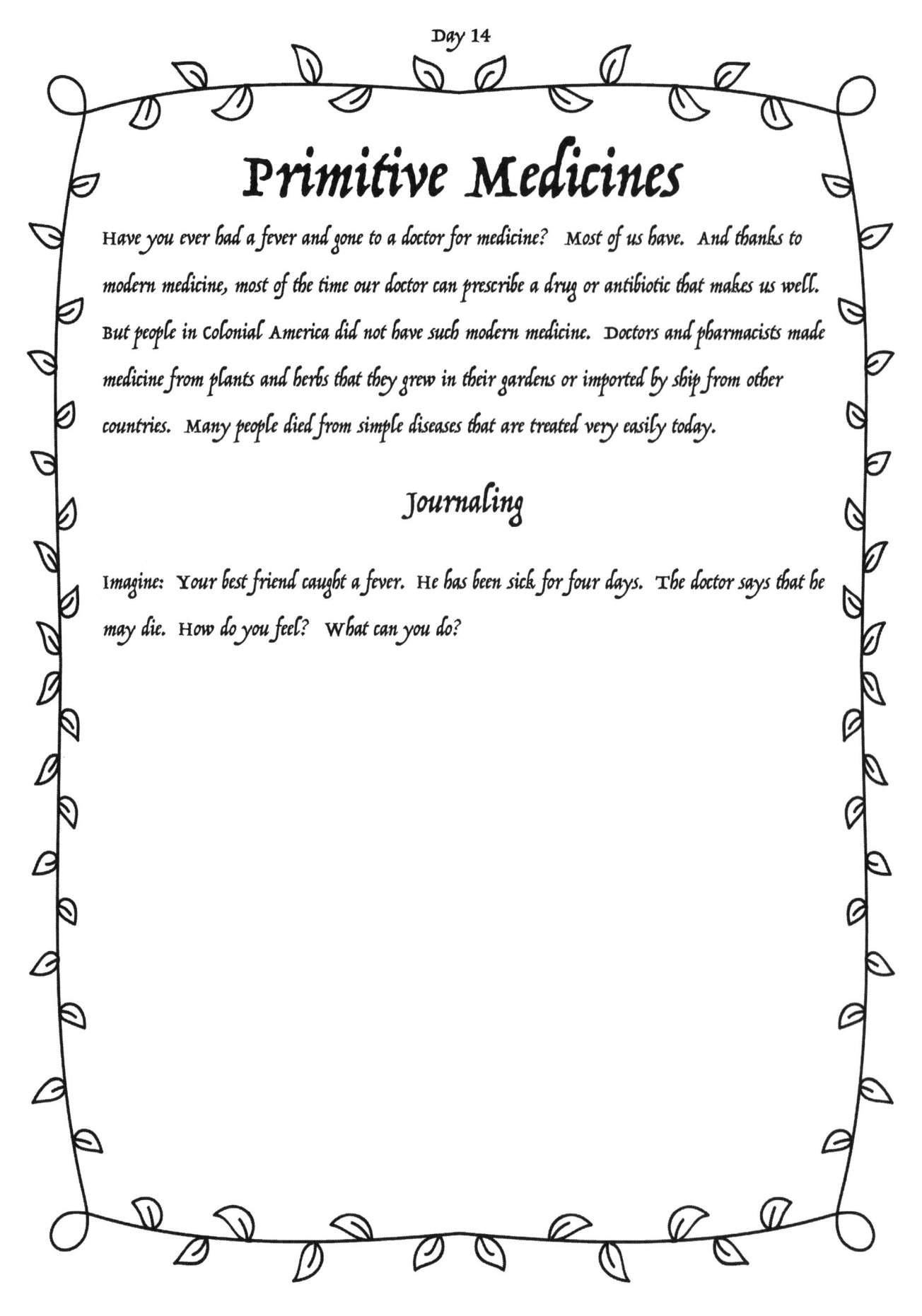

Primitive Medicines

Have you ever had a fever and gone to a doctor for medicine? Most of us have. And thanks to modern medicine, most of the time our doctor can prescribe a drug or antibiotic that makes us well. But people in Colonial America did not have such modern medicine. Doctors and pharmacists made medicine from plants and herbs that they grew in their gardens or imported by ship from other countries. Many people died from simple diseases that are treated very easily today.

Journaling

Imagine: Your best friend caught a fever. He has been sick for four days. The doctor says that he may die. How do you feel? What can you do?

Day 14

Primitive Medicines

Look online or in a book and discover one plant that was used for medicine in Colonial times.

Describe how that plant was used to treat diseases, and then draw a picture of the plant.

Day 15

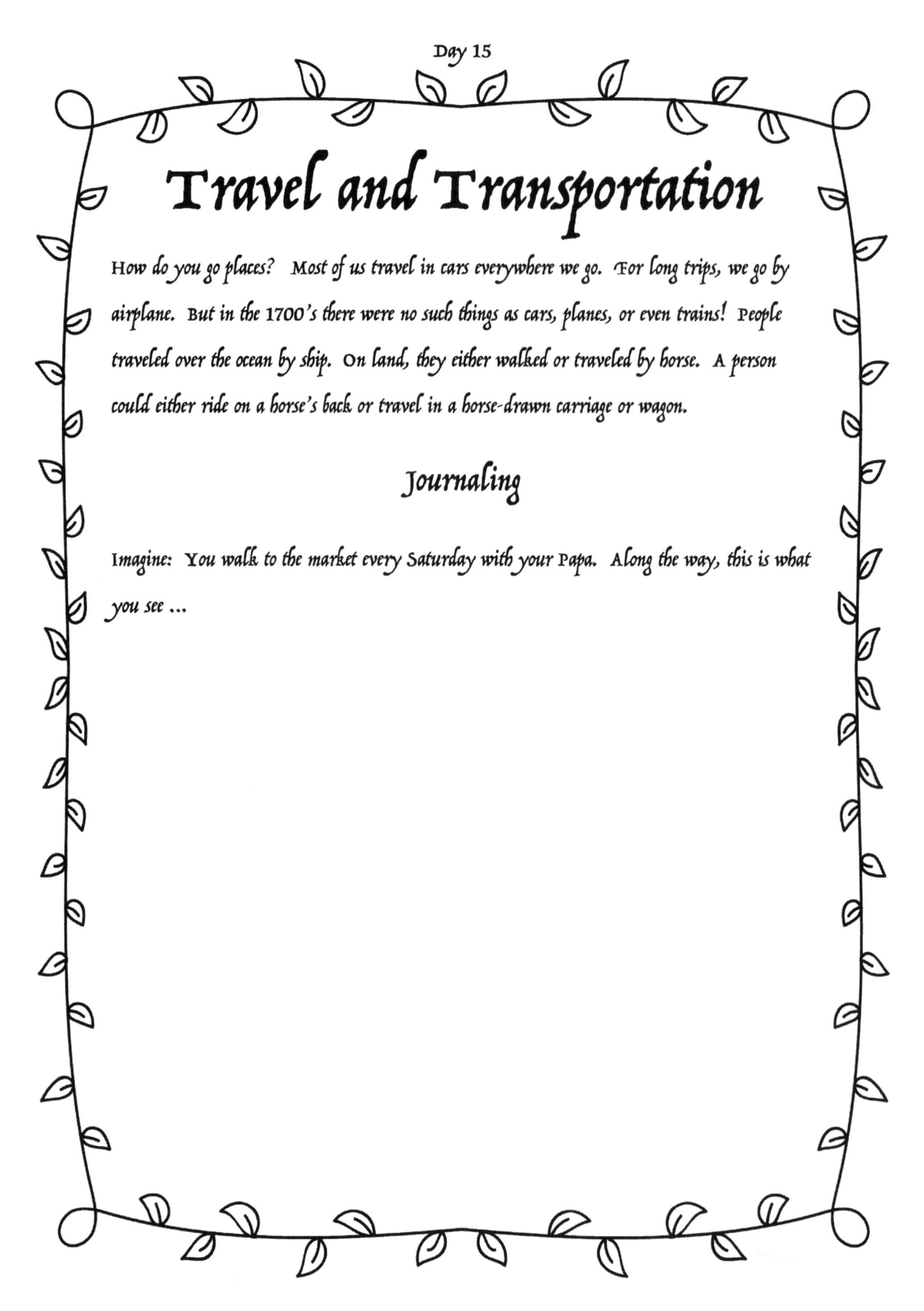

Travel and Transportation

How do you go places? Most of us travel in cars everywhere we go. For long trips, we go by airplane. But in the 1700's there were no such things as cars, planes, or even trains! People traveled over the ocean by ship. On land, they either walked or traveled by horse. A person could either ride on a horse's back or travel in a horse-drawn carriage or wagon.

Journaling

Imagine: You walk to the market every Saturday with your Papa. Along the way, this is what you see ...

Day 15

Travel and Transportation

Day 16

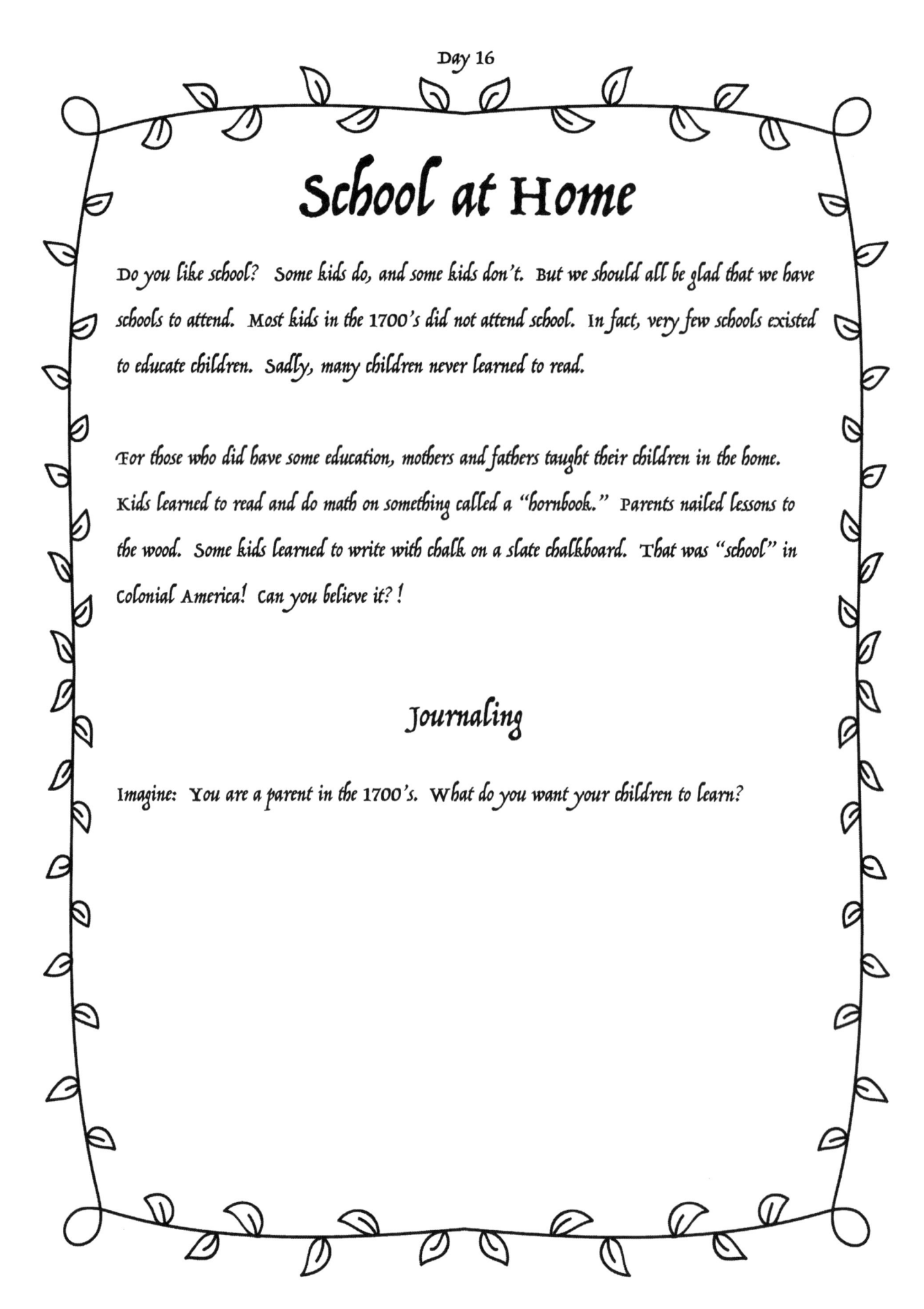

School at Home

Do you like school? Some kids do, and some kids don't. But we should all be glad that we have schools to attend. Most kids in the 1700's did not attend school. In fact, very few schools existed to educate children. Sadly, many children never learned to read.

For those who did have some education, mothers and fathers taught their children in the home. Kids learned to read and do math on something called a "hornbook." Parents nailed lessons to the wood. Some kids learned to write with chalk on a slate chalkboard. That was "school" in colonial America! Can you believe it?!

Journaling

Imagine: You are a parent in the 1700's. What do you want your children to learn?

Day 16

School at Home

TODAY'S ASSIGNMENT: Write a poem about life in the 1700's.

Day 17

Strange Dishes

Do you have a favorite plate or cup or bowl? Most of us do. Maybe it is because you have had that particular dish since you were very small. Maybe it is a cup that has your name on it. But, even though we might have our favorite dishes, our cupboards are filled with all kinds of dishes for eating. Most homes have dozens (maybe even hundreds) of plates, bowls, cups, saucers, and glasses!

But, if you had been living during Colonial/Revolutionary War times, you probably would have only owned a single bowl, cup, and plate. Dishes were expensive. Most were made of a heavy metal called pewter. Sometimes people on the frontier made their own dishes out of wood. Some people even made cups and spoons out of cow's horns! Their forks looked very strange, as well. Instead of having four prongs, most Colonial forks only had two!

Journaling

Imagine: You eat your meals from a wooden plate and a pewter bowl. You eat with a wooden spoon and a two-pronged fork. You drink your milk from a cow's horn cup. Describe what it is like to eat with these very strange dishes …

Day 17

Strange Dishes

Day 18

Toys, Games, and Dolls

What kind of games do you play? Most kids today enjoy video games and have a closet full of other games and toys. But little girls in Colonial America had no such games to play. There were no factories that made toys. Many children simple roamed in the forests and fields for entertainment. They played with family pets, and with one another. If a Colonial girl had a toy to play with, it was because her mother or father made it.

Most girls enjoyed playing with a doll. That doll was often a Colonial girl's very best friend. Though there were some fancy, expensive dolls in the big cities, most Colonial girls played with homemade dolls. Their mothers made their dolls out of scraps of cloth or corn shucks. They had stuffed heads, or sometimes heads that their fathers carved out of wood.

Journaling

Imagine: You are a Colonial girl. Your only toy is a doll. Your doll is special because …

Day 18

Toys, Games, and Dolls

Make a list of materials that you would use to build your own homemade doll. Draw a picture of a doll that you would like to make. For a really fun project, work with your mother or grandmother over the next week to make your very own homemade Colonial American doll!

Day 19

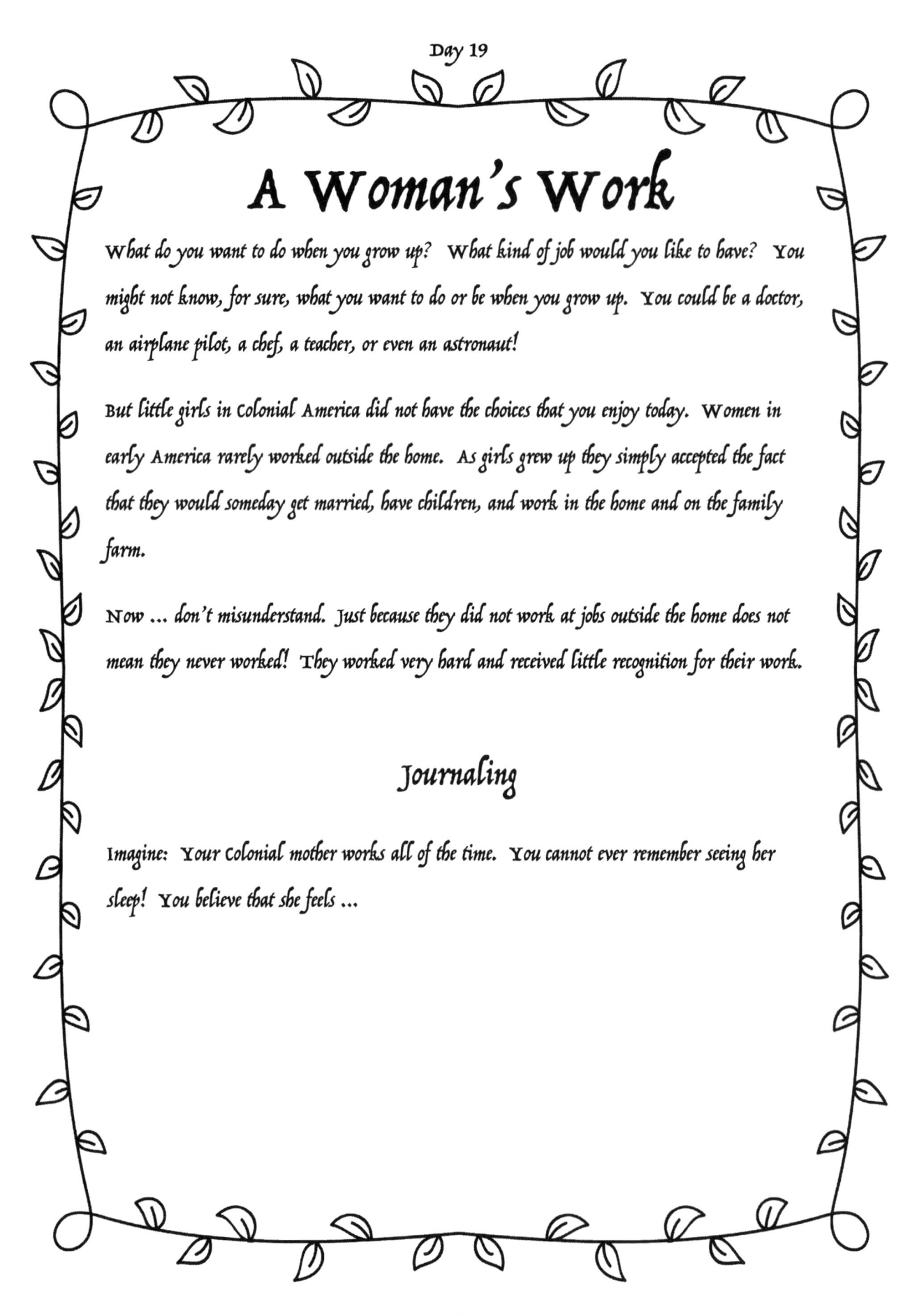

A Woman's Work

What do you want to do when you grow up? What kind of job would you like to have? You might not know, for sure, what you want to do or be when you grow up. You could be a doctor, an airplane pilot, a chef, a teacher, or even an astronaut!

But little girls in Colonial America did not have the choices that you enjoy today. Women in early America rarely worked outside the home. As girls grew up they simply accepted the fact that they would someday get married, have children, and work in the home and on the family farm.

Now ... don't misunderstand. Just because they did not work at jobs outside the home does not mean they never worked! They worked very hard and received little recognition for their work.

Journaling

Imagine: Your Colonial mother works all of the time. You cannot ever remember seeing her sleep! You believe that she feels ...

Day 19

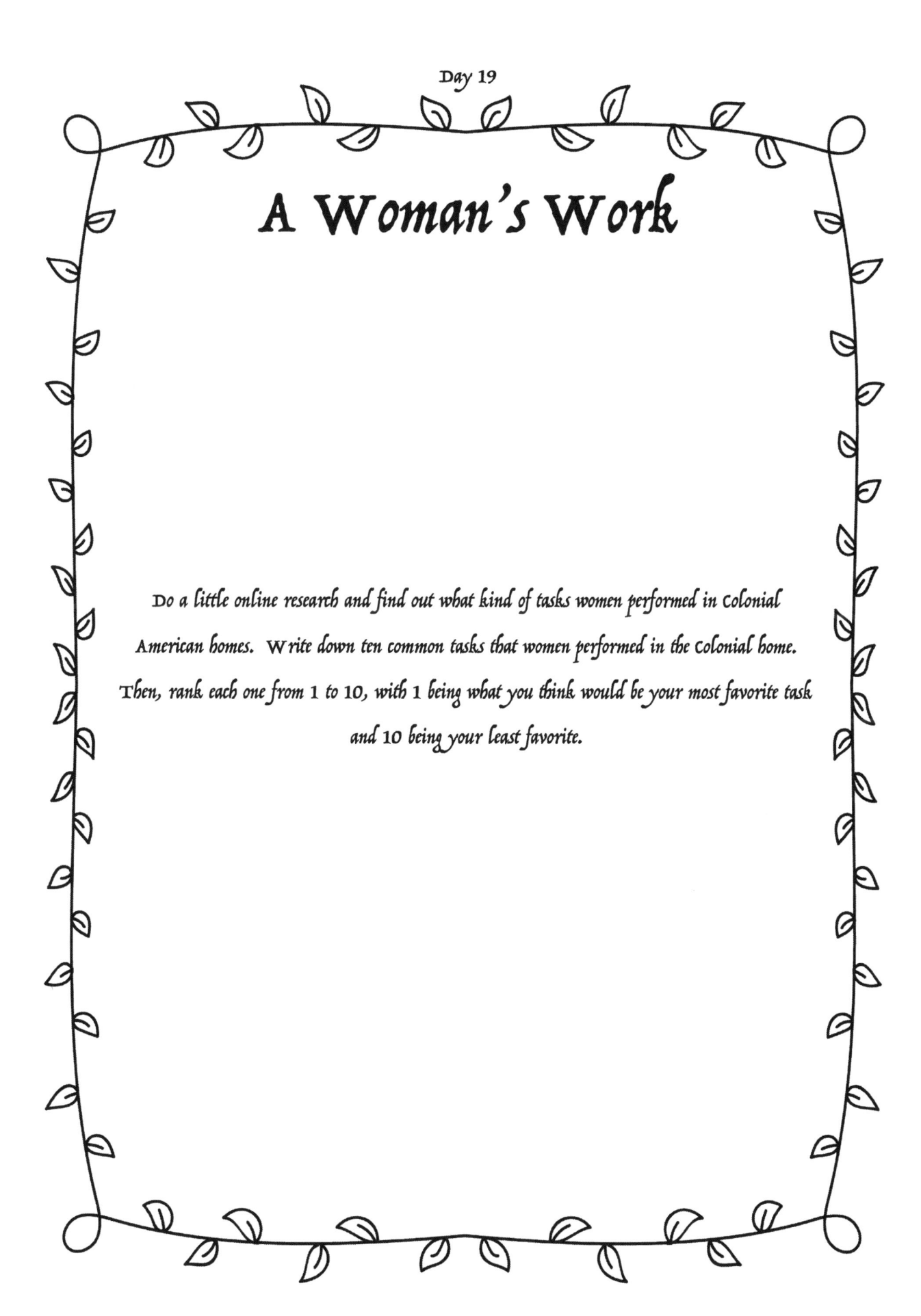

A Woman's Work

Do a little online research and find out what kind of tasks women performed in Colonial American homes. Write down ten common tasks that women performed in the Colonial home. Then, rank each one from 1 to 10, with 1 being what you think would be your most favorite task and 10 being your least favorite.

Day 20

Diary Day

It's our weekly diary day! Pretend that you are living in Colonial America. Try to imagine yourself living during that time. Now ... write two diary pages as a Colonial girl. Reflect on the things you have learned over the past week about the colonial life of a young girl.

Day 20

Diary Day

Day 21

My Short Story

Today you will write a Short Story! You have three pages to tell a story about a little girl in colonial America. Let your imagination run wild!

Day 21

Day 21

American Revolution

Harsh Life on the Homefront

Day 22

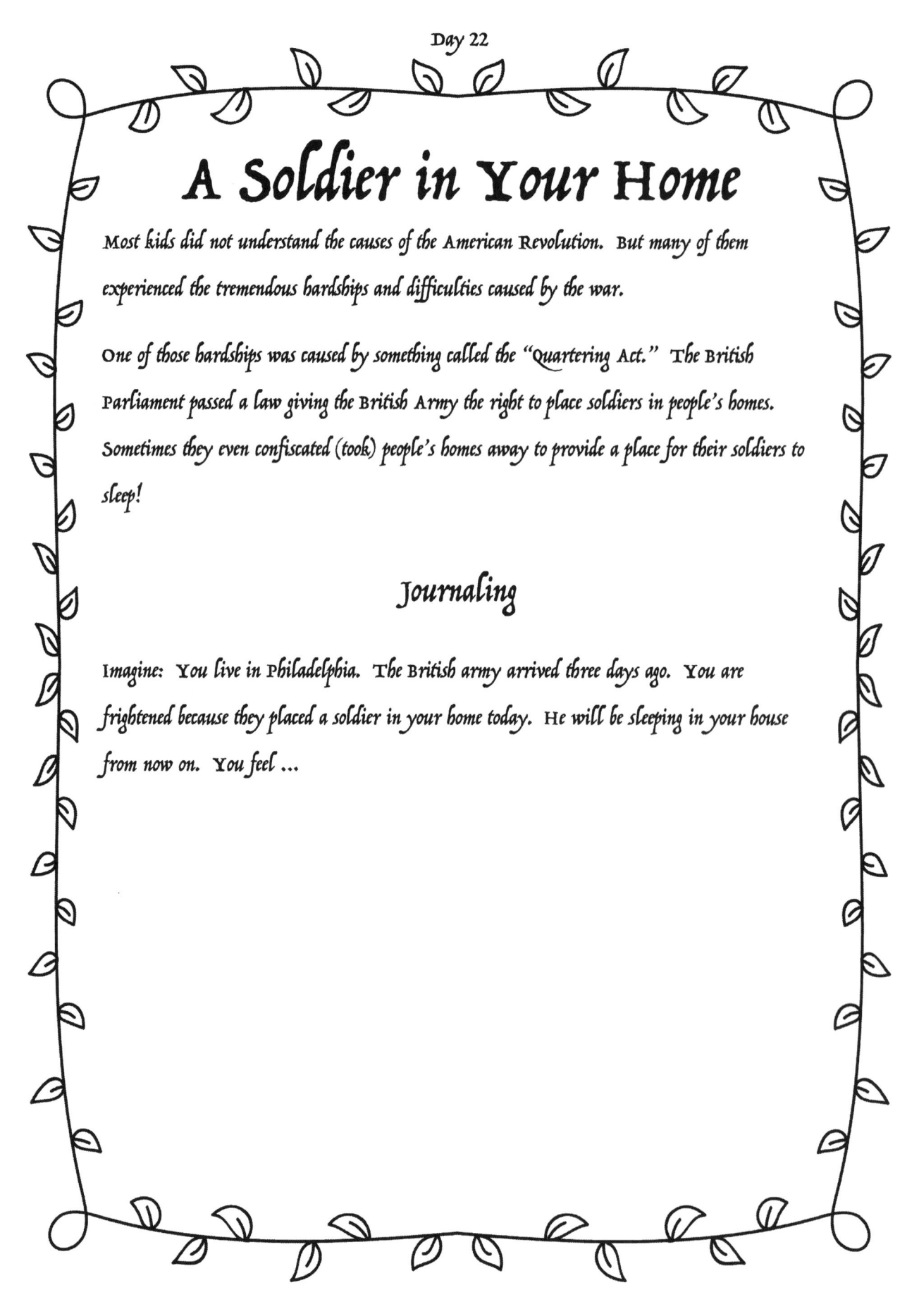

A Soldier in Your Home

Most kids did not understand the causes of the American Revolution. But many of them experienced the tremendous hardships and difficulties caused by the war.

One of those hardships was caused by something called the "Quartering Act." The British Parliament passed a law giving the British Army the right to place soldiers in people's homes. Sometimes they even confiscated (took) people's homes away to provide a place for their soldiers to sleep!

Journaling

Imagine: You live in Philadelphia. The British army arrived three days ago. You are frightened because they placed a soldier in your home today. He will be sleeping in your house from now on. You feel …

Day 22

A Soldier in Your Home

Draw a British "Redcoat" Soldier

Day 23

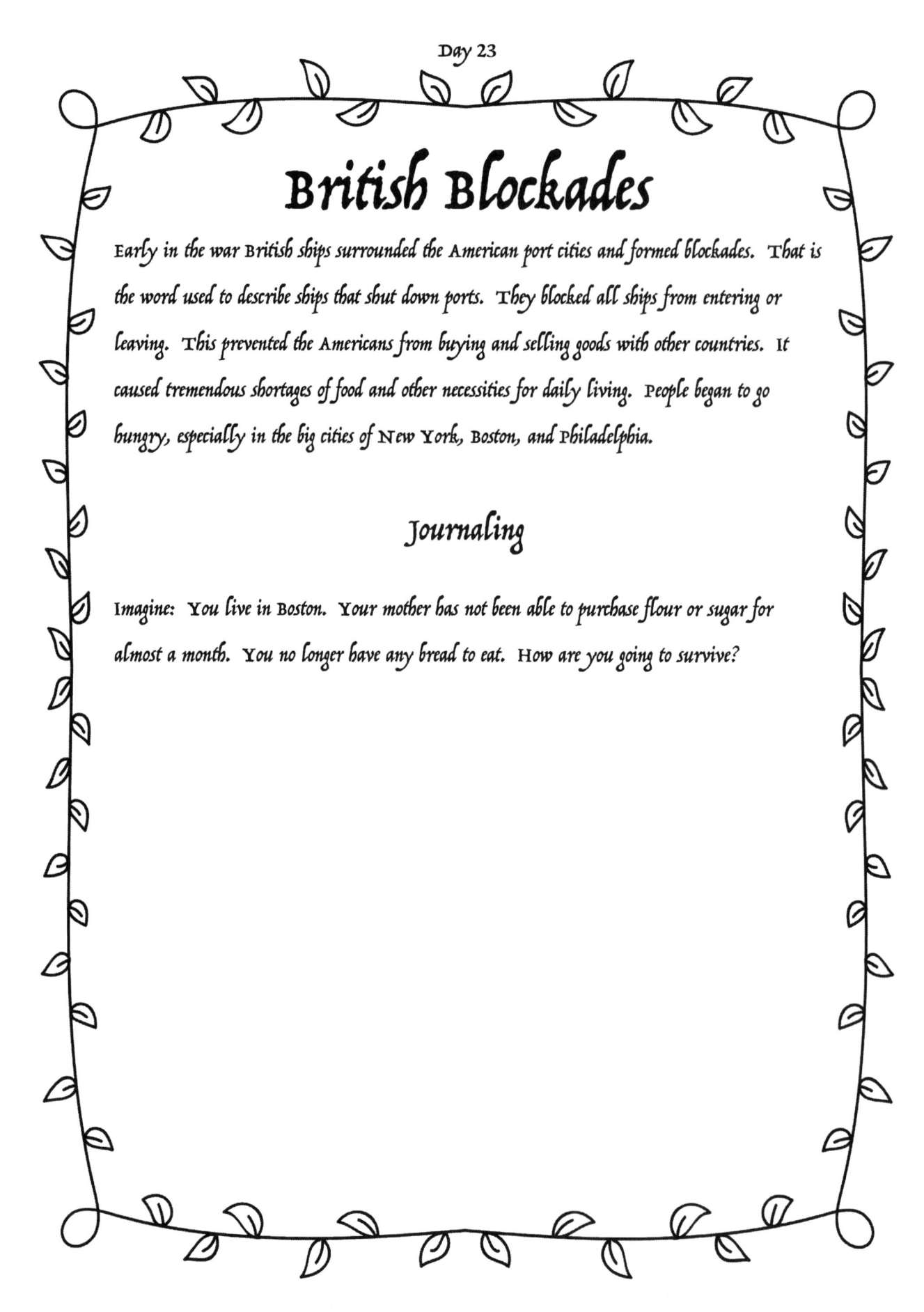

British Blockades

Early in the war British ships surrounded the American port cities and formed blockades. That is the word used to describe ships that shut down ports. They blocked all ships from entering or leaving. This prevented the Americans from buying and selling goods with other countries. It caused tremendous shortages of food and other necessities for daily living. People began to go hungry, especially in the big cities of New York, Boston, and Philadelphia.

Journaling

Imagine: You live in Boston. Your mother has not been able to purchase flour or sugar for almost a month. You no longer have any bread to eat. How are you going to survive?

Day 23

British Blockades

Day 24

The Suffering Cities

When the food ran out and there were no more jobs in the big cities, people had very few options. Many of them fled the cities and went into the countryside in search of work and food. They had to leave their homes and find friends or relatives in small villages to live with. Some had to build cabins or shacks in the forests. The children of these families were often cold and hungry. Some had to walk many miles.

Journaling

Imagine: Your Papa just told you that this is the last night in your home. There is no more food in New York City. You must all go to your uncle's farm on Long Island. You have lived in the city your entire life. You have never even visited a farm! What will it be like?

Day 24

The Suffering Cities

Day 25

Papa is a Soldier

Many thousands of men served in the Continental Army or in the state militias during the American Revolution. The militia soldiers usually served only a few months, but those who served in the Continental Army were often gone for a year or more. Mail service was unreliable. Many American wives heard no word from their husbands for months at a time. They often did not know if their soldier husband was dead or alive!

Journaling

Imagine: Your father is a sergeant in the Connecticut Continental Line. He marched off to war two years ago. You have not received a letter from him in over six months. You wonder what he is doing right now. Maybe he is ...

Papa is a Soldier

Day 26

Brother is a Militiaman

Most people do not know that many teen-aged boys served as soldiers in the American Revolution. Sometimes all boys fifteen and over were required to serve in the militia. These boys fought to defend their homes. Sometimes they stood beside their fathers and uncles and fought in big battles. Sometimes they did not come back home.

Journaling

Imagine: Your fifteen-year-old brother served as a soldier in the Rowan County, North Carolina, Militia. Last year he left with the other soldiers to fight a battle in South Carolina at a place called Camden. Your family recently received a letter informing you that he is a prisoner and is being held on a British prison ship in Charlestown Harbor. What do you think his life is like on that prison ship?

Day 26

Brother is a Militiaman

Draw an 18th century sailing ship that might have been used to hold prisoners.

Day 27

Slaves

Some Colonial American families owned slaves. Slavery was a system in which one human being could actually own another human being. In America, most slaves were from Africa. They were treated as property, which included being bought and sold. Sometimes families were separated and children taken from their mothers when they were sold to other slave owners.

Journaling

Imagine: Your father owns four slaves. They include a man and a woman and two children ... a little boy and a little girl. The girl is your age. Your father is thinking about selling her because he needs more money. How does that make you feel? What would you say to your father?

Day 27

Slaves

Day 28

Diary Day

It's our weekly diary day! Pretend that you are living during the Revolutionary War. Try to imagine the challenges that you would encounter during that time. Now ... write two diary pages as a Colonial girl.

Day 28

Diary Day

Day 29

Refugees

In some parts of early America during the Revolution, soldiers even committed acts of war against ordinary people ... civilians. This was particularly true in the state of Georgia. Local militias made up of men who were loyal to England would sometimes burn down the homes of the American Patriot militiamen who were fighting for independence. Likewise, the militiamen who fought against the British and their Loyalist allies would sometimes burn down the homes of their Loyalist neighbors. When people were forced out of their homes like that, they became refugees. Many thousands of people hid in the forests of Georgia and South Carolina to escape their enemies.

Journaling

Imagine: You live on the Georgia frontier near the town of Augusta. Your papa is away from home serving in the war. You were awakened during the night by the sounds of screaming and breaking glass. Your mother helped you and your brothers and sisters escape your burning cabin. You are hiding in the woods and watching your cabin burn. What are you going to do now?

Day 29

Refugees

Draw a picture of a cabin burning on the frontier during the Revolution.

Day 30

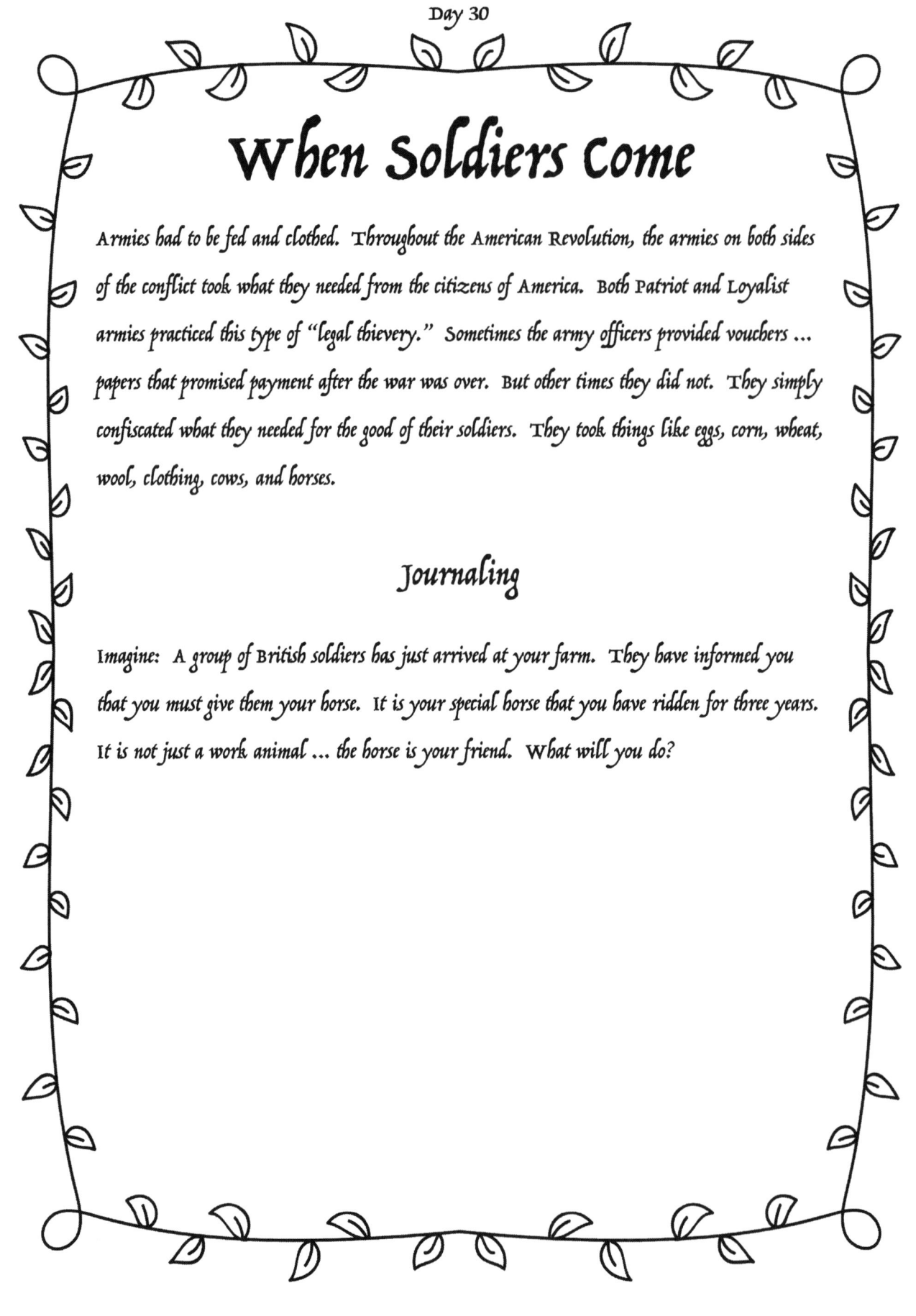

When Soldiers Come

Armies had to be fed and clothed. Throughout the American Revolution, the armies on both sides of the conflict took what they needed from the citizens of America. Both Patriot and Loyalist armies practiced this type of "legal thievery." Sometimes the army officers provided vouchers ... papers that promised payment after the war was over. But other times they did not. They simply confiscated what they needed for the good of their soldiers. They took things like eggs, corn, wheat, wool, clothing, cows, and horses.

Journaling

Imagine: A group of British soldiers has just arrived at your farm. They have informed you that you must give them your horse. It is your special horse that you have ridden for three years. It is not just a work animal ... the horse is your friend. What will you do?

Day 30

When Soldiers Come

Day 31

Helping the War Effort

Women and children in America did many things to help soldiers serving in the war. They sewed clothing and flags, cooked meals, and cared for the wounded. Sometimes they even helped in the fighting by loading muskets, rolling cartridges (paper tubes with gunpowder and a musket ball inside), making bandages, or carrying water. When their husbands and fathers were off serving in the war, the women and children helped the war effort by growing gardens and growing farm crops. They did the things that the men would be doing if they were at home!

Journaling

If I had lived through the American Revolution, I would have helped win America's independence by ...

Day 31

Helping the War Effort

Day 32

Fighting the Indians

Not all American soldiers fought against British or Loyalist armies. Many Indians, native Americans who lived in various tribes throughout the frontier, often took the side of the British. The Indians desperately wanted to keep American settlers from moving across the Appalachian Mountains and building homes on their land. The area that we now know as Kentucky was once part of Virginia. Many people have no idea that battles in the Revolution took place in Kentucky! But it was a particularly violent and bloody place during the war. Everyone who lived in the frontier settlements in Kentucky had to fight against the Indians to protect their homes and their lives.

Journaling

Imagine: You live at a Kentucky fort called Bryan Station. Over five hundred natives and British soldiers have surrounded the fort. There are only forty men to fight against the huge army of Indians. How can you help them?

Day 32

Fighting the Indians

Battle in Your Back Yard

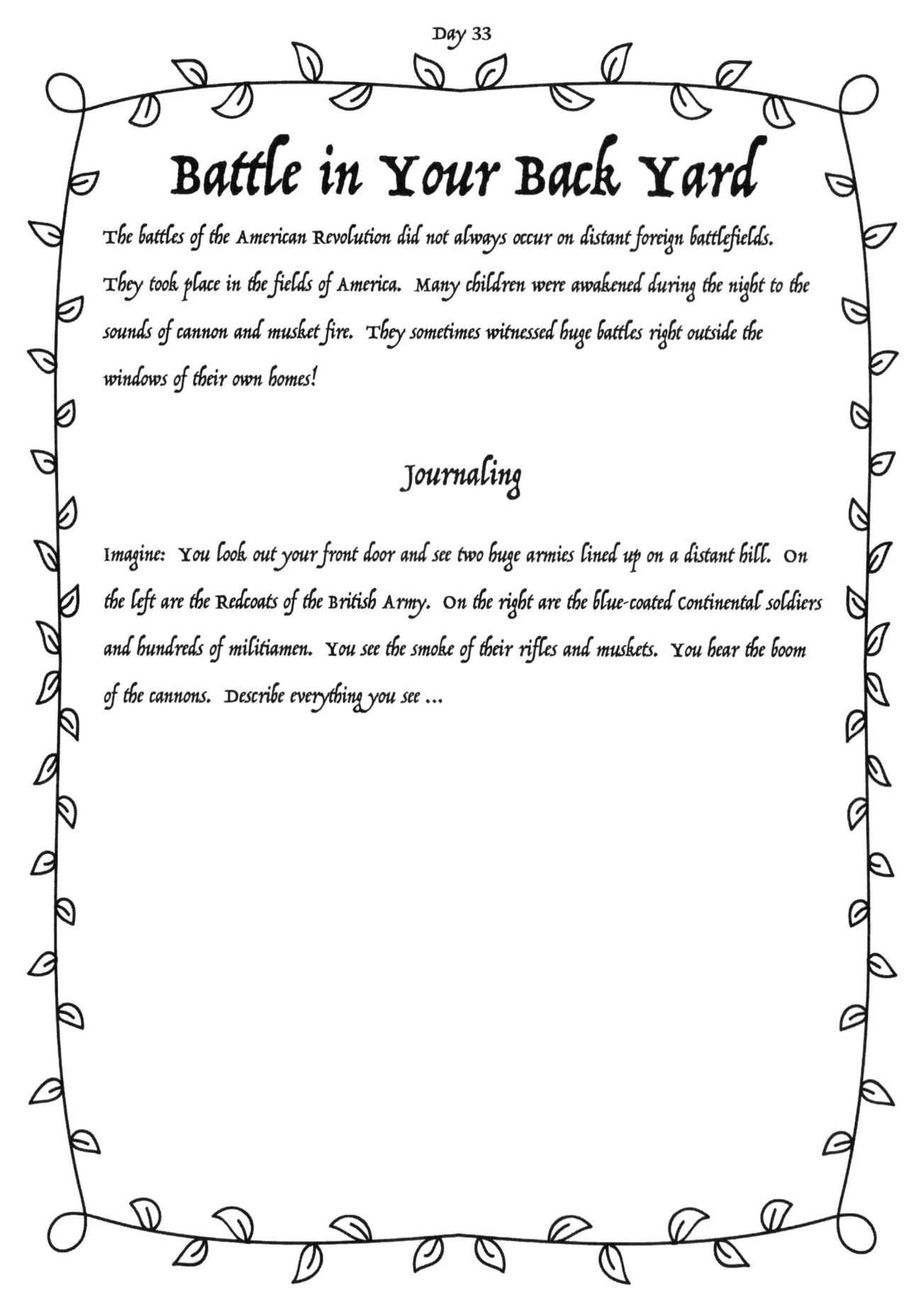

The battles of the American Revolution did not always occur on distant foreign battlefields. They took place in the fields of America. Many children were awakened during the night to the sounds of cannon and musket fire. They sometimes witnessed huge battles right outside the windows of their own homes!

Journaling

Imagine: You look out your front door and see two huge armies lined up on a distant hill. On the left are the Redcoats of the British Army. On the right are the blue-coated Continental soldiers and hundreds of militiamen. You see the smoke of their rifles and muskets. You hear the boom of the cannons. Describe everything you see ...

Battle in Your Back Yard

Write a poem to describe the battle near your home.

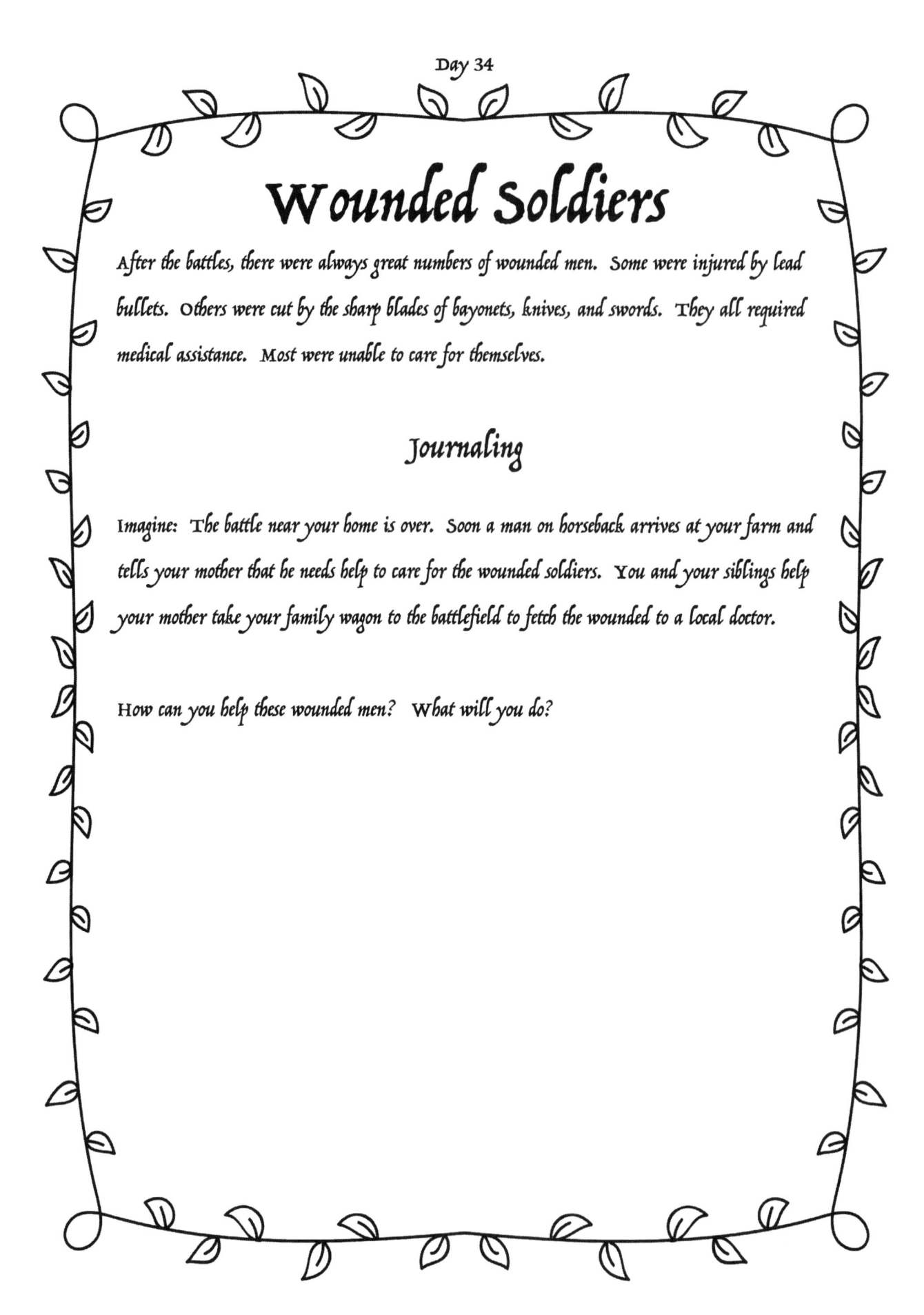

Wounded Soldiers

After the battles, there were always great numbers of wounded men. Some were injured by lead bullets. Others were cut by the sharp blades of bayonets, knives, and swords. They all required medical assistance. Most were unable to care for themselves.

Journaling

Imagine: The battle near your home is over. Soon a man on horseback arrives at your farm and tells your mother that he needs help to care for the wounded soldiers. You and your siblings help your mother take your family wagon to the battlefield to fetch the wounded to a local doctor.

How can you help these wounded men? What will you do?

Day 34

Wounded Soldiers

Day 35

Diary Day

It's our weekly diary day! Pretend that you are living during the Revolutionary War. Try to imagine yourself living during that time. Now ... write two diary pages as a Colonial girl.

Day 35

Diary Day

My Next Short Story

Today you will write another Short Story! You have three pages to tell a story about a little girl in America whose father was serving in the American Revolution. You choose the location (state) where she lived. Tell about the difficulties that she faced. Tell her story!

Day 36

Day 36

American Revolution

Your History

The Boston Tea Party

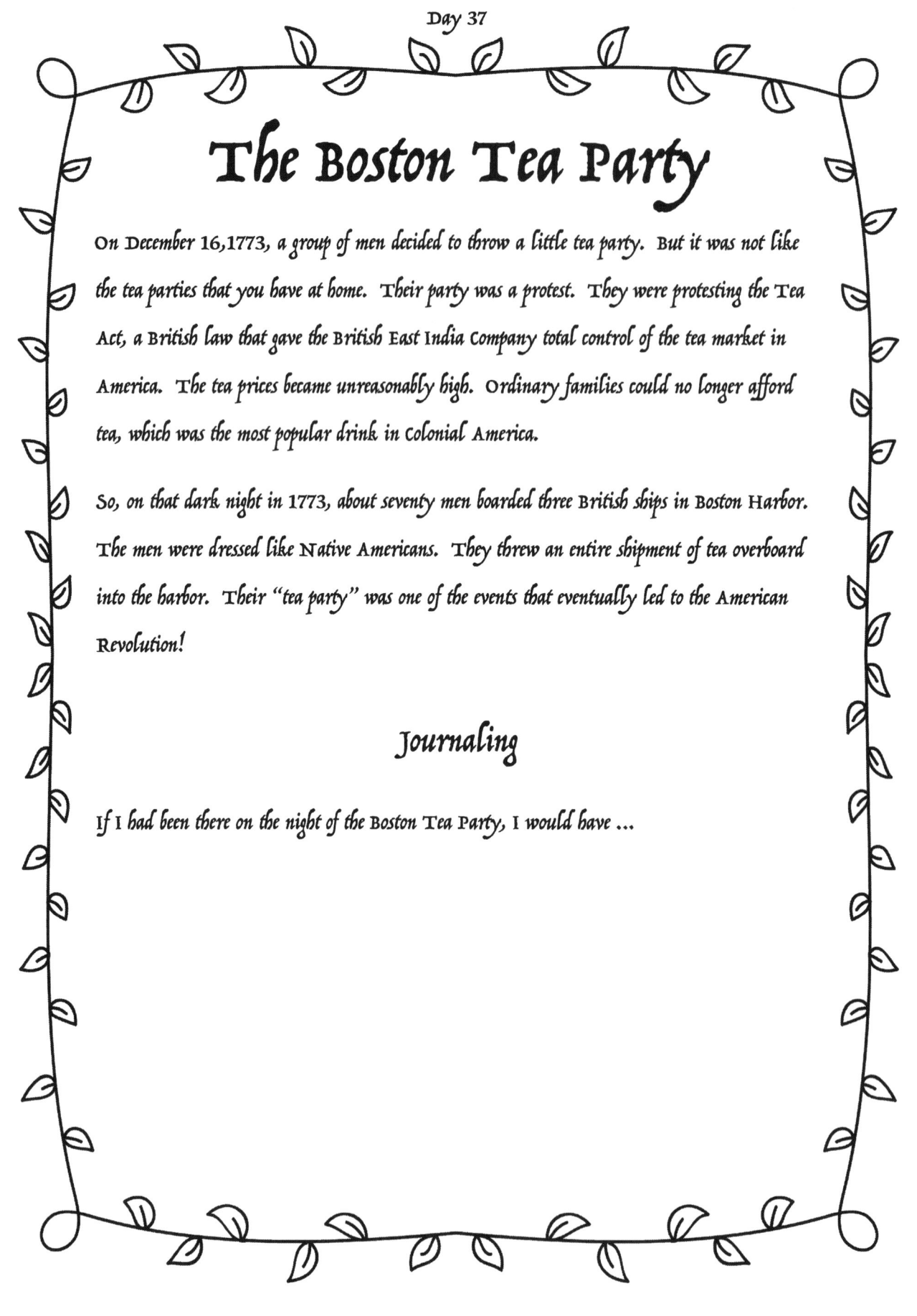

On December 16, 1773, a group of men decided to throw a little tea party. But it was not like the tea parties that you have at home. Their party was a protest. They were protesting the Tea Act, a British law that gave the British East India Company total control of the tea market in America. The tea prices became unreasonably high. Ordinary families could no longer afford tea, which was the most popular drink in Colonial America.

So, on that dark night in 1773, about seventy men boarded three British ships in Boston Harbor. The men were dressed like Native Americans. They threw an entire shipment of tea overboard into the harbor. Their "tea party" was one of the events that eventually led to the American Revolution!

Journaling

If I had been there on the night of the Boston Tea Party, I would have …

The Boston Tea Party

Day 38

A Shot Heard 'Round the World

Boston, Massachusetts, was a hotbed of rebellion against England. Many people there grew to resent the soldiers who were stationed there to keep watch over the people and maintain control over the city. Some men of Boston who were part of the "Sons of Liberty" began to gather guns and ammunition and hide them in villages outside of Boston. They were preparing for war!

On April 19, 1775, over seven hundred British troops left Boston. They were going to the village of Concord to seize rebel supplies of gunpowder and weapons. When they reached the village of Lexington they encountered seventy militiamen known as "Minutemen" waiting for them. There was a brief standoff between the two opposing groups.

Then someone fired a shot. No one knows which side shot first. But that brief firefight became known as the "Shot Heard 'Round the World." It was the first battle of the American Revolution!

Journaling

Imagine: You were watching from the window of your home in Lexington. You saw seventy brave Minutemen standing in the field opposite the seven hundred red-coated troops of His Majesty's British Army. Describe the scene in detail. What did you see? What did you hear? How did you feel?

Day 38

A Shot Heard 'Round the World

Day 39

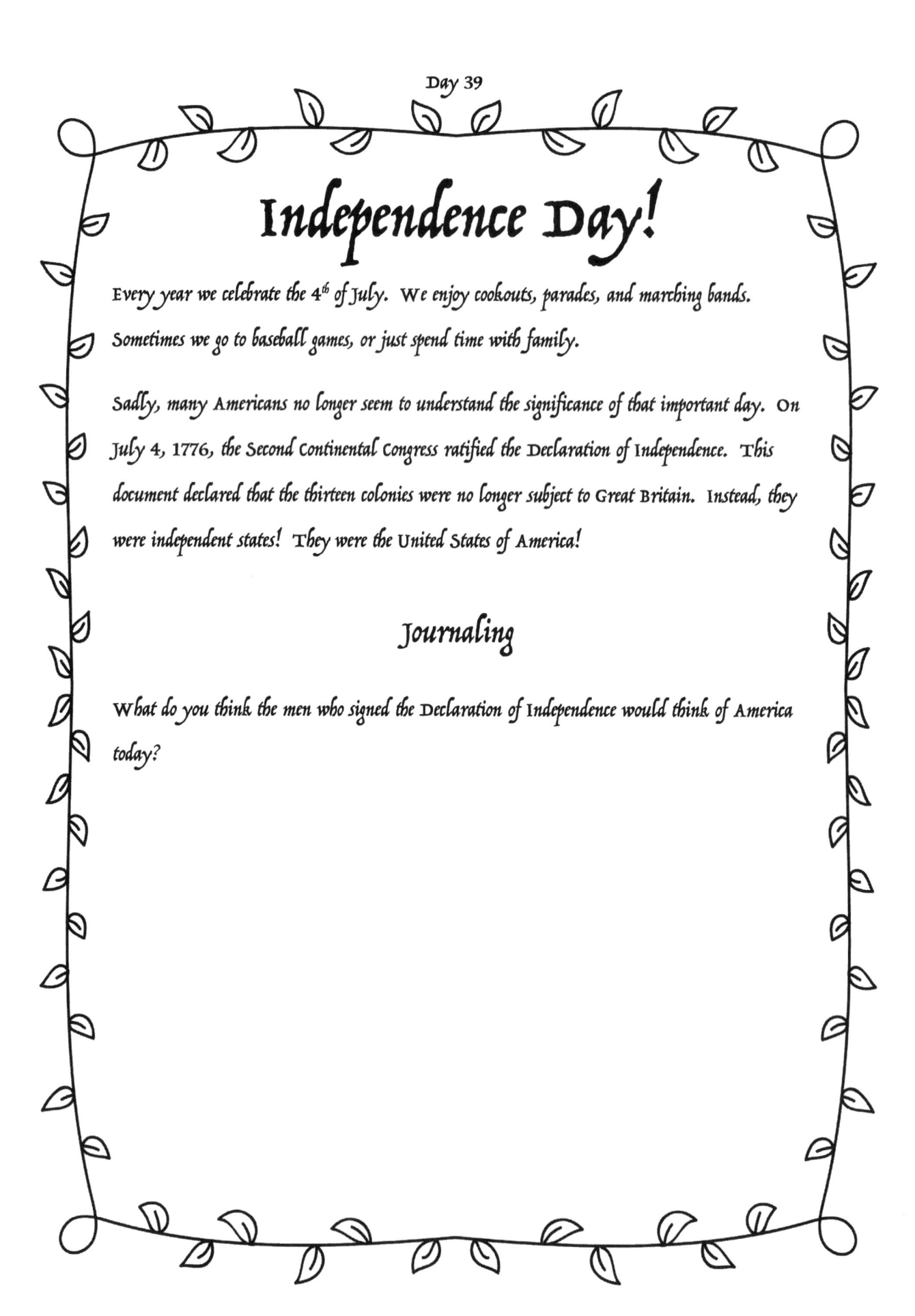

Independence Day!

Every year we celebrate the 4th of July. We enjoy cookouts, parades, and marching bands. Sometimes we go to baseball games, or just spend time with family.

Sadly, many Americans no longer seem to understand the significance of that important day. On July 4, 1776, the Second Continental Congress ratified the Declaration of Independence. This document declared that the thirteen colonies were no longer subject to Great Britain. Instead, they were independent states! They were the United States of America!

Journaling

What do you think the men who signed the Declaration of Independence would think of America today?

Day 39

Independence Day!

Draw a picture of your family celebrating Independence Day!

Day 40

George Washington

Many people call George Washington the "Father of Our Country." In many ways, it is a title that he very much deserves. He accepted the commission of the Continental Congress to become the Commanding General of the armies of the United States. He led that army through its many defeats and victories. He was steadfast in his courage and in his faithfulness to our new nation. Then, when the war was over, he became our first president in 1789! Truly, he was the "Father of Our Country!"

Journaling

If you had the chance to meet George Washington, what would you ask him?

Day 40

George Washington

Draw a portrait of George Washington.

Day 41

Valley Forge

The Continental Army was not doing well in the winter of 1777-1778. General Washington took his army into a winter camp at a famous place called Valley Forge, Pennsylvania. The soldiers built small cabins and huts and settled down to wait for springtime.

But the winter at Valley Forge was one of the most difficult experiences that most of those soldiers ever faced. It was very cold and snowy. The worst part, though, was the lack of food. There was almost nothing to eat in the entire region. The combatting armies had consumed all of the crops and livestock. The local people were not willing to share what little they had with the Continental Army. So, the men suffered tremendously from hunger, cold, and disease. Almost 2,000 men died in that cold encampment.

Journaling

Imagine: Your family lives on a farm near Valley Forge. You can see the suffering of the soldiers there. Every day soldiers wander onto your family farm in search of something to eat. They have no shoes on their feet and are dressed in tattered rags. What could you do to help them?

# Valley Forge

Diary Day

It's our weekly diary day! Pretend that you are living during the Revolutionary War. Try to imagine yourself living during that time. Now ... write two diary pages as a Colonial girl.

Day 42

Diary Day

Our French Allies

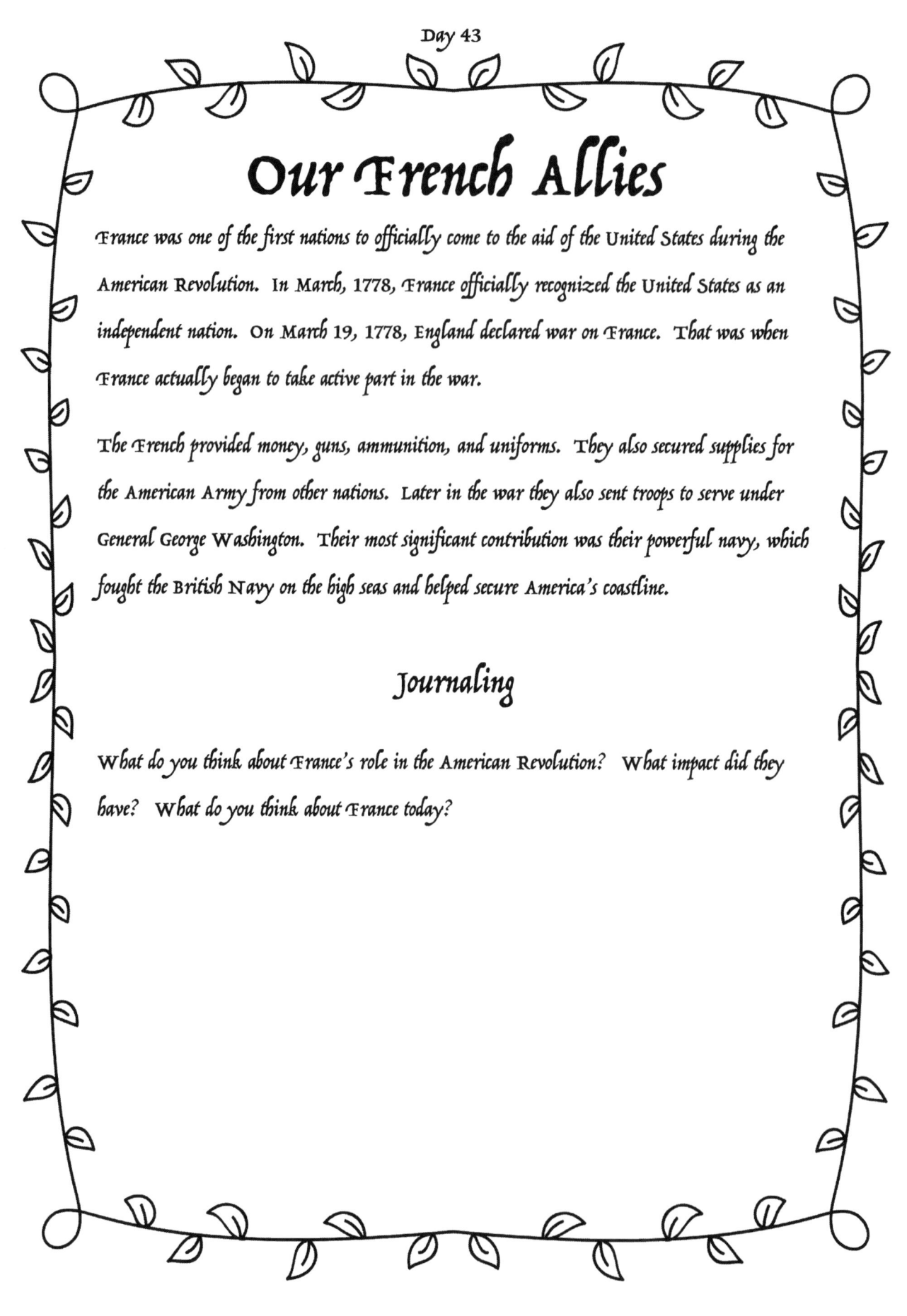

France was one of the first nations to officially come to the aid of the United States during the American Revolution. In March, 1778, France officially recognized the United States as an independent nation. On March 19, 1778, England declared war on France. That was when France actually began to take active part in the war.

The French provided money, guns, ammunition, and uniforms. They also secured supplies for the American Army from other nations. Later in the war they also sent troops to serve under General George Washington. Their most significant contribution was their powerful navy, which fought the British Navy on the high seas and helped secure America's coastline.

Journaling

What do you think about France's role in the American Revolution? What impact did they have? What do you think about France today?

Day 43

Our French Allies

Do some research and find out what the flag of France looked like in 1778. Draw a picture of that French flag.

Benedict Arnold - Traitor

Not everyone who originally fought for American Independence remained true to the cause. Some soldiers walked away from the battlefield and returned to their homes. The army called them, "deserters," because they abandoned and deserted their fellow soldiers. It was actually a crime to be a deserter. The penalty was very harsh.

Other people were not just deserters. Some were traitors to the cause. They actually changed sides! The most infamous one was General Benedict Arnold. He was a famous Continental Army general. He was well-known for his bravery on the battlefield. But he was frustrated and felt that he did not get the attention and promotions that he deserved. So, on September 21, 1780, he actually changed sides and became a general in the British Army! He is America's most famous traitor! In our country, his name has actually become synonymous with the word traitor.

Journaling

Have you ever had a friend desert or betray you? Write about that experience. Write about how it made you feel, and how you responded to the situation.

Benedict Arnold - Traitor

Day 45

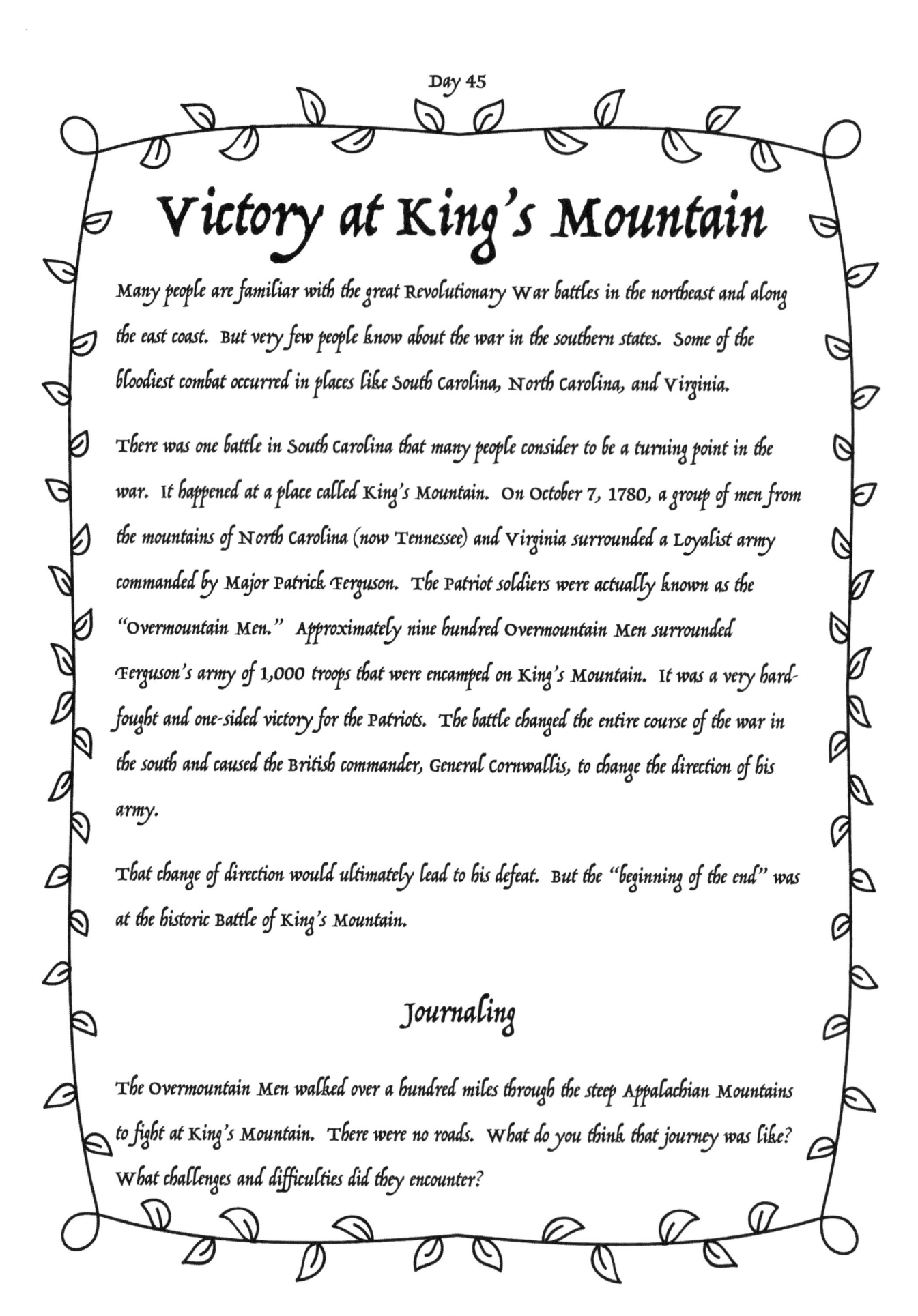

Victory at King's Mountain

Many people are familiar with the great Revolutionary War battles in the northeast and along the east coast. But very few people know about the war in the southern states. Some of the bloodiest combat occurred in places like South Carolina, North Carolina, and Virginia.

There was one battle in South Carolina that many people consider to be a turning point in the war. It happened at a place called King's Mountain. On October 7, 1780, a group of men from the mountains of North Carolina (now Tennessee) and Virginia surrounded a Loyalist army commanded by Major Patrick Ferguson. The Patriot soldiers were actually known as the "Overmountain Men." Approximately nine hundred Overmountain Men surrounded Ferguson's army of 1,000 troops that were encamped on King's Mountain. It was a very hard-fought and one-sided victory for the Patriots. The battle changed the entire course of the war in the south and caused the British commander, General Cornwallis, to change the direction of his army.

That change of direction would ultimately lead to his defeat. But the "beginning of the end" was at the historic Battle of King's Mountain.

Journaling

The Overmountain Men walked over a hundred miles through the steep Appalachian Mountains to fight at King's Mountain. There were no roads. What do you think that journey was like? What challenges and difficulties did they encounter?

Victory at King's Mountain

Day 46

The War is Over!

British General Cornwallis made a bad choice when he took his army from North Carolina into Virginia. He wanted to locate a deep-water port on the Virginia coast where he could bring ships and troops from New York City to reinforce his army. He decided to go to a place called Yorktown, located on a little peninsula of land on the Atlantic coast.

What he did not know was that General George Washington had found out about his location and secretly moved his army from the north. Washington cut off Cornwallis by land. And then, quite unexpectedly, our French allies arrived with a fleet of ships and several thousand troops. They cut off Cornwallis from the sea.

General Lord Cornwallis was completely surrounded. The Americans and French bombarded the British and kept them under siege for three weeks. Finally, on October 19, 1781, Cornwallis surrendered. The surrender ended most combat between the armies in America. The official end of the war came on September 3, 1783, with the signing of the Treaty of Paris. The war was over!

Journaling

Imagine: You live in a small village in North Carolina. A messenger on horseback rides into your town proclaiming, "Cornwallis has surrendered! The war is over!" What happens in your town? How do the people react? How does your family celebrate the victory?

Day 46

The War is Over!

Day 47

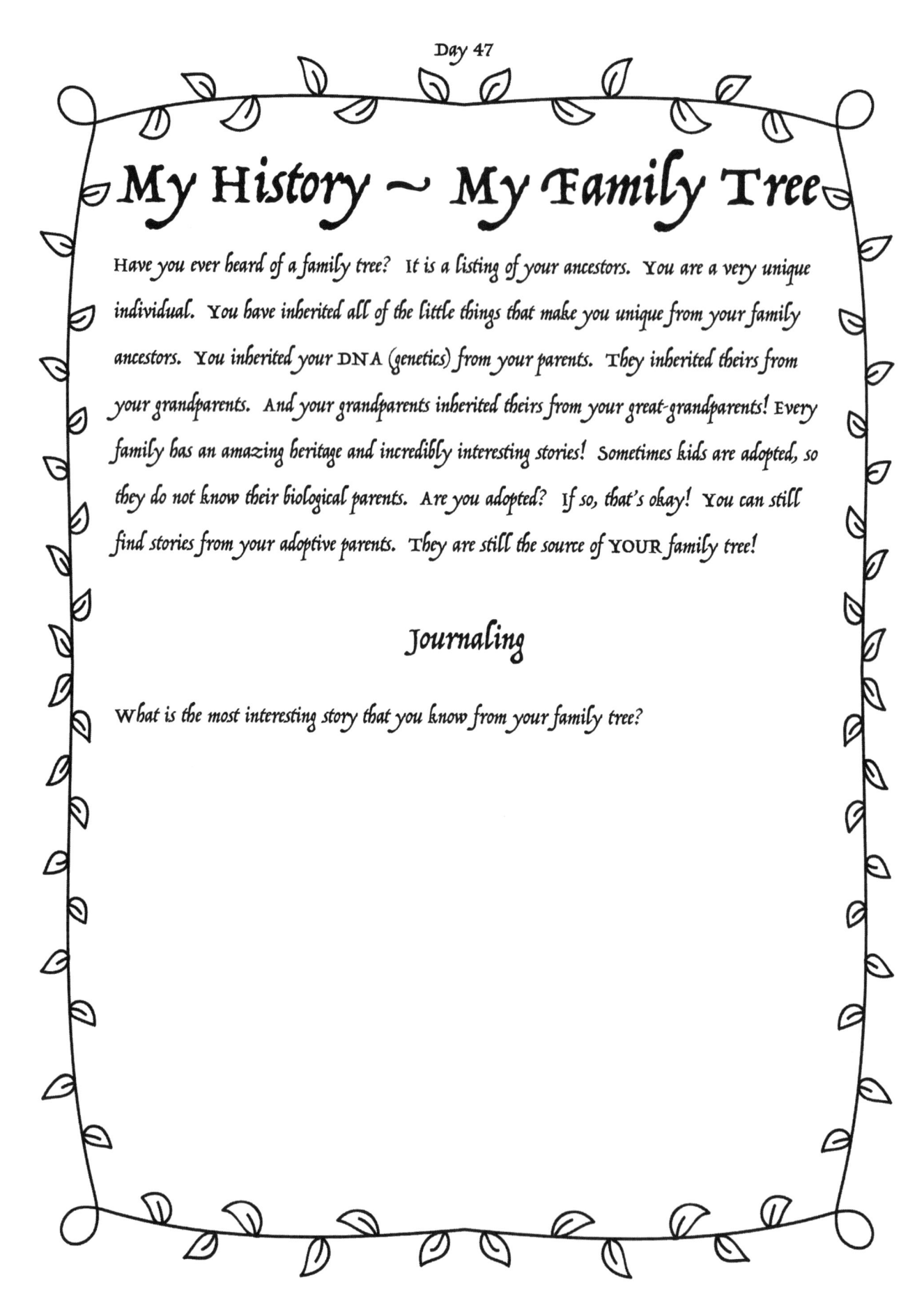

My History ~ My Family Tree

Have you ever heard of a family tree? It is a listing of your ancestors. You are a very unique individual. You have inherited all of the little things that make you unique from your family ancestors. You inherited your DNA (genetics) from your parents. They inherited theirs from your grandparents. And your grandparents inherited theirs from your great-grandparents! Every family has an amazing heritage and incredibly interesting stories! Sometimes kids are adopted, so they do not know their biological parents. Are you adopted? If so, that's okay! You can still find stories from your adoptive parents. They are still the source of YOUR family tree!

Journaling

What is the most interesting story that you know from your family tree?

Day 47

My History ~ My Family Tree

Write the names of the people in YOUR Family Tree!

Me _____

Mom _____   Dad _____

Grandmother - _____
Grandfather - _____

Grandmother - _____
Grandfather - _____

Day 48

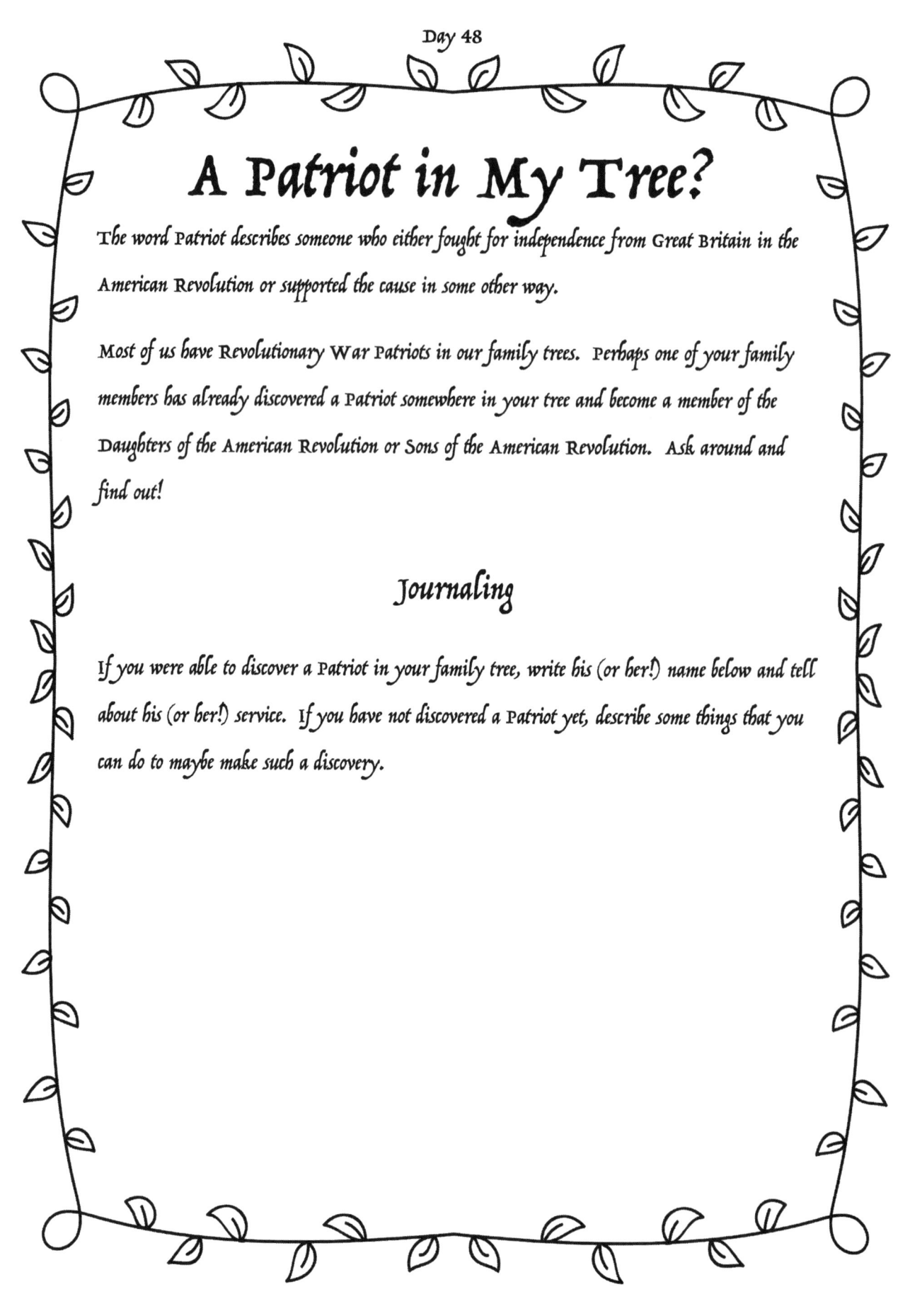

A Patriot in My Tree?

The word Patriot describes someone who either fought for independence from Great Britain in the American Revolution or supported the cause in some other way.

Most of us have Revolutionary War Patriots in our family trees. Perhaps one of your family members has already discovered a Patriot somewhere in your tree and become a member of the Daughters of the American Revolution or Sons of the American Revolution. Ask around and find out!

Journaling

If you were able to discover a Patriot in your family tree, write his (or her!) name below and tell about his (or her!) service. If you have not discovered a Patriot yet, describe some things that you can do to maybe make such a discovery.

Day 48

A Patriot in My Tree?

Color the Continental Soldier!

Day 49

Diary Day

This is your last Diary Day! Write about the unusual or surprising things that you have learned about the American Revolution this week.

Day 49

Diary Day

Day 50

My Short Story MASTERPIECE

On the next few pages I want to encourage you to write your MASTERPIECE! Write a short story about anything that interests you in the Colonial or Revolutionary War periods. Be detailed and descriptive. Help your readers experience your story. This will be your most challenging entry in this journal. So, make it a GREAT STORY!

When you are finished, I want to encourage you to get your parents to help you type your story and then submit it for the annual MY COLONIAL JOURNAL SHORT STORY CONTEST. I will select one winner each calendar year. The winner will receive a set of free books and have their story featured on mycolonialjournal.com.

SUBMITTING YOUR STORY

Email your MASTERPIECE to

cockedhatpublishing@mail.com

Day 50

Day 50

Day 50

Day 50

Day 50

Other Books by Geoff Baggett

My Colonial Journal For Boys

PATRIOT KIDS OF THE AMERICAN REVOLUTION SERIES

Little Hornet

Little Warrior

Little Spy of Vincennes

KENTUCKY FRONTIER ADVENTURES

A Bucket Full of Courage: Betsy Johnson of Bryan Station

A Note From the Author

I hope you enjoyed your MY COLONIAL JOURNAL experience! It has been my desire to help you connect with and enjoy early American history.

Please let me know about your experience! Go to www.mycolonialjournal.com and tell me about it. I have created a blog where parents and kids can share their experiences and stories. I look forward to meeting you there!

Also, please encourage your parents to write a review for this book on Amazon.com. Thank you!

Geoff Baggett

About the Author

Geoff Baggett is a historical researcher and author with a passion for all things Revolutionary War. He is an active member of the Sons of the American Revolution and the Descendants of Washington's Army at Valley Forge. Geoff has discovered over twenty American Patriot ancestors in his family tree.

He is an avid living historian, appearing regularly in period clothing and uniforms in classrooms, reenactments, and other commemorative events. He lives with his family on a quiet little place in the country in rural western Kentucky.

Made in the USA
Middletown, DE
14 May 2017